W9-BDV-018

ICONIC

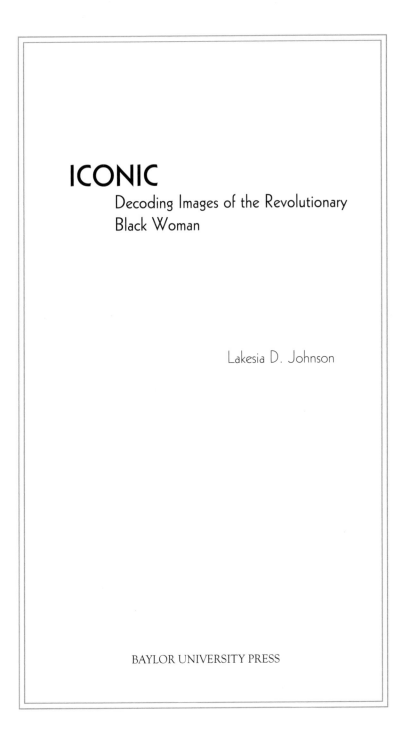

ICONIC
Decoding Images of the Revolutionary Black Woman

Lakesia D. Johnson

BAYLOR UNIVERSITY PRESS

Cover Design by *the*BookDesigners
Cover Image modified from stock art ©Shutterstock/Roi Brooks
Book Design by Diane Smith

Library of Congress Cataloging-in-Publication Data

Johnson, Lakesia D.
  Iconic : decoding images of the revolutionary Black woman / Lakesia D. Johnson.
   183 p. cm.
  Summary: "A visual and narrative iconography of the Black female revolutionary across a variety of media texts and historical contexts"-- Provided by publisher.
  Includes bibliographical references and index.
  ISBN 978-1-60258-644-4 (hardback)
  1. Women, Black--United States--History. 2. African American women--United States. 3. Women revolutionaries--United States--History. I. Title.
  E185.86.J6433 2012
  305.48'896073--dc23

                    2012007880

Printed in the United States of America on acid-free paper with a minimum of 30% pcw recycled content.

Dedicated to my parents,
Jerrie L. Hatten and Luddie Hatten Sr.

Thank you for your prayers,
unconditional love, and support.

TABLE OF CONTENTS

ACKNOWLEDGMENTS

First and foremost, I want to acknowledge my mother, Jerrie L. Hatten, for always believing that I could do great things, even when I was clinging to life as a preemie and the doctors had given up hope. Thank you for your strength, tenacity, persistence, and refusal to let anyone block your success or the success of your children. I'd also like to thank my many friends and family whose understanding and support propelled me forward during those times when I wanted to give up.

A very special thank you to my editor, Carey C. Newman, Gladys S. Lewis, Jenny Hunt, Jordan Rowan Fannin, and all the members of Team Baylor UP for your patience, encouragement, and guidance. This book couldn't have happened without you. I also want to thank Katya Gibel Mevorach for your enthusiasm and support of me and this project from the very beginning.

Shanna Greene Benjamin, Karla Erickson, Michelle Nasser, and Angela Onwuachi-Willig, thank you for reading early drafts of my manuscript and being the best colleagues, sistah-friends, and writing buddies that a girl could ask for. I also want to thank Sylvea Hollis for spending days with me in the coffee shop when I needed company. Thanks to members of the Grinnell College English Department and the Gender, Women's & Sexuality

x   Studies Program, especially Astrid Henry and Heather Lobban-Viravong for your encouragement, mentoring, and support of my scholarship.

The seeds of this book were planted when I was a graduate student at The Ohio State University. I want to thank Judith Mayne, Terry Moore, Valerie Lee, and Ruby Tapia for your mentoring and encouragement during the early stages of this project. I'd also like to thank Valora Blackson and Megan Chawansky for your support and encouragement.

1

THE MYTH OF THE ANGRY BLACK WOMAN
From Sojourner Truth to Michelle Obama

On October 8, 2008, Larry King interviewed Mrs. Michelle Obama. The interview took place after her husband, Barack Obama, had secured the Democratic nomination for president and was in the midst of a very nasty campaign waged by Republican nominee John McCain. After showing a clip from the most recent interview between Obama and McCain, in which McCain refers to Obama as "that one," King proceeded to question Mrs. Obama about anger. During the interview, King asked Mrs. Obama if she was upset about the way that others treated her husband and even asked whether Barack Obama became angry with such actions. Mrs. Obama assured King that her husband does not get angry about the back and forth that happens in politics. King's persistent probing implied the question that most African American women have been confronted with but never like to answer, "Are you angry?"

King was focused on exposing some deeply repressed anger that, presumably, was being disguised by Mrs. Obama. Tim Graham—not a Barack Obama supporter[1]—analyzed this interview in his article "Larry King Kept Asking Michelle Obama: 'Attack Dog' Palin Doesn't Make You Mad?" and noted that King posed "13 anger-management questions in all."[2] Graham's

2   observation is significant because it raises an important dilemma faced by black women. The question, "Are you angry?" or "Are you mad?" is a loaded one, recalling long-standing fears and negative images of strong black women.

Throughout the history of the United States, African American people have struggled, having been represented as savage, ignorant, and deserving of deplorable treatment, and black women in particular have been portrayed as angry and uncontrollable.[3] Mrs. Obama was directly confronting this image of black womanhood in her interview with Larry King. As a highly educated professional, Mrs. Obama certainly knew about the stereotype of the angry black woman and was aware that she could easily be cast as one if she handled the situation in the "wrong" way.[4]

Later in the interview, King questioned Mrs. Obama about comments made by then–vice presidential candidate Sarah Palin that alleged that Barack Obama had been "palling around with terrorists." Mrs. Obama redirected the conversation and assured King that she was not angry and that Palin's comments were just politics. In fact, she explained that she had not seen the footage of Palin because the demands of her schedule did not permit her time to watch television. After showing her a clip of Palin's speech, King pursued the following line of questioning:

> *King:* That don't get you any mad?
> *M. Obama:* You know, fortunately, I don't watch it.
> *King:* Oh, well now you've seen it.
> *M. Obama:* I've seen it.
> *King:* Alright. She said your husband pals around with terrorists. And she's referring to William Ayers, I guess. Do you know William Ayers?
> *M. Obama:* Yes. Yes. Yes. Barack served on the board of the Annenberg Challenge with Bill Ayers and. . . .
> *King:* That was started by the Annenberg family, right?
> *M. Obama:* Absolutely. And Mrs. Annenberg, in fact, endorsed John McCain. So I don't know anyone in Chicago who's heavily involved in education policy who

doesn't know Bill Ayers. But, you know, again, I go back to the point that, you know, the American people aren't asking these questions.

King: You don't think that it affects the campaign?

M. Obama: You know, I think that we've been in this for twenty months and people have gotten to know Barack. He's written books. Books have been written about him. He, like all of the other candidates [has] been thoroughly vetted. And I think people know Barack Obama. They know his heart, they know his spirit. And the thing that I just encourage people [to do] is to judge Barack and judge all of these candidates based on what they do, their actions, their character, what they do in their lives, rather than what somebody did when they were eight, or six years old.

King: When someone calls, and says [who's running for vice president] that your husband associates with terrorism, that upsets you, I would think.

M. Obama: You know that's part of politics. But . . .

King: It doesn't—it goes right off of you?

M. Obama: You know—these issues have come up before. But the one thing that I'm proud about with Barack is that one of the things he's been talking about is our tone. And it's the notion that he says we can disagree without being disagreeable. And that's, you know, where he's trying to get to in this campaign, the notion that we can disagree on some fundamental issues in this country, but we have to do it without demonizing one another, without labeling one another, because we're in some tough times now. And what we can see from the fall of this economy is that when we fall, we all fall. And when we rise, we all rise. And whether we're Republicans or Democrats or Independents, or black or white or straight or gay, and that we're in this together and that there are times that we will disagree, that we won't share the same policies. But, we're gonna rise and fall together. And that's the tone that I like. And I think that's where Americans want their elected officials to be.

King: So you bear her no umbrage?

M. Obama: Not at all. Not at all. I mean, that's not where we need to be right now. I mean, we need to be at a point where we're figuring out how to work together, again, whether we agree or disagree . . .

King continued the interview by asking Mrs. Obama what she thinks of Sarah Palin. Mrs. Obama praised Palin as a model of a woman balancing work and family. She said,

> You know, I think she provides an excellent example of all the different roles that women can and should play. . . . I'm a mother with kids and I've had a career and I've had to juggle. She's doing publicly what so many women are doing on their own privately. And what we're fighting for is to make sure that all women have the choices that Sarah Palin and I have to make these decisions and do it without hurting their families. . . . And we're in a position now, as I go across the country and I've had conversations with working women and many find that they have to do the juggling, but, they're doing it without the support. They're living in communities where jobs have dried up, so, their family members have had to move away so they can't rely on mothers and all those informal support structures. . . . So what Sarah Palin and I have that all women deserve is the choice and the resources to make their choices work. And I think that's what we need to fight for.

King next asked, "And the senator shares that view?" to which Mrs. Obama responded,

> Absolutely—I mean he's seen—you know Barack has grown up with strong women. He's seen me. He grew up in a household where his grandmother was the primary breadwinner. He saw her juggling to support the entire family, saw her working her way up from being a secretary at a bank to being a senior official. His mother was a single parent. He saw her struggle in many ways. He's seen the struggles of women and knows that there's an inequity there and that we're still in this country dealing with pay equity issues for women.

In the close questioning by Larry King, Mrs. Obama not only averted dangerous campaign questions about anger but also effectively separated herself from stereotypical images of the "angry black woman" that King's questions invoked. In so doing, she created a powerful image of herself as a supportive wife, a peacemaker, a strong advocate of working women and their families and represented herself as a woman who (like other women) struggled to balance the demands of work and family. Mrs. Obama's answers also revealed her husband as a supporter of women's rights, as one who, by watching the struggles of strong women in his life, came to understand the persistence of gender inequality in this country. Through this exchange with her seasoned questioner, Mrs. Obama resisted any attempt to cast her and her husband as angry blacks, while simultaneously affirming her strength as a strong professional black woman.

The exchange between King and Mrs. Obama illustrates the essence of *Iconic*. This book asks what it means to represent black womanhood and explores how these representations are connected to a long history of representational depictions and choices that communicate the role of black women in social movements. On the one hand, *Iconic* explores how representations of strong, revolutionary black women within popular culture are used to reinforce dominant, lingering, and mostly negative stereotypes about black women, stereotypes much like the one King depended upon when he relentlessly questioned Mrs. Obama about whether she was angry. On the other hand, *Iconic* traces the numerous ways that African American women activists, actors, writers, and musicians have negotiated, confronted, and resisted stereotypical representations of black womanhood by taking control of their public images and constructing iconic depictions of and narratives about African American womanhood. Like Mrs. Obama did when she recast herself and her husband's campaign, these revolutionary black women have used these counterimages to promote a vision of racial and gender justice that is attentive to their intersectional

6 experiences and committed to movements that fight against racism, sexism, and other forms of oppression.[5] Avoiding a direct response to King was indeed a savvy, strategic, and political move. In her answers, Mrs. Obama resisted the stereotypical construction of her as an angry black woman by affirming the American political process, Sarah Palin's shared struggles to balance family and work, and her and Barack Obama's commitment to social justice for all. The campaign could have been very different had she succumbed to King's baiting.

Considering that Barack Obama was campaigning for the most important office in the United States, plenty was at stake. Not only would he be president, he would be the first African American president. All eyes were on him and his family. The idea of a *Black* family in the *White* House was beyond what many imagined could be possible in America. And it is a certainty that an angry black woman could never be successfully assimilated into the image of the ideal first lady. Mrs. Obama had to walk a fine line. She had to show that she was a strong supporter of her husband, while simultaneously showing true allegiance to the United States. She had to be supportive of Barack, while simultaneously promoting an image of herself and her family as patriotic and good for the country. She also had to fight stereotypical representations of black women.[6]

In the interview with Larry King, Mrs. Obama circumvented his attempts to place her into the angry, oversensitive, loud, and dangerous black woman box. Instead she stayed focused. When she emphasized her husband's tone and contrasted it with the negative tone coming from the opposing party, she created an image of racial cooperation and affinity that is in direct opposition to the image of racial distrust and antagonism that the image of the stereotypical angry black woman promotes.[7] In fact, her brilliant response to King diffused his attempt to define her. She successfully resisted the angry black woman stereotype and replaced it with an image of herself and her husband as patriotic Americans filled with "righteous anger" about the existence of inequality and injustice. If Mrs. Obama and her husband were angry about anything, it certainly was not anger about petty name-calling. Like other Americans, they were angry about losing soldiers in the war and watching corrupt bankers get rich while the rates of poverty and unemployment rose. She replaced the image of a mythological dangerous and angry black woman with a portrait of an American whose legitimate and righteous anger about injustice was appropriate given the current state of the country. Mrs. Obama managed to discuss anger in a way that reduced the negative impact that long-cherished stereotypes about strong black women could have had on the 2008 campaign. Unfortunately, she would later be confronted with the reemergence of the stereotype of the angry and difficult black woman during her husband's reelection campaign in 2012.[8]

The need to negotiate and manage her image, in the face of numerous stereotypes about black womanhood, is neither new nor unique to Mrs. Obama. Black women have been confronting, resisting, and subverting stereotypical representations for a long time.[9] For example, important civil rights activists Ida B. Wells and Sojourner Truth had to be concerned with how they represented themselves, and were represented, while they worked for black people within an all-white American legal and social context that refused to give them full citizenship.[10] Sojourner Truth, formerly Isabella Baumfree, was born into slavery, was forced to claim her freedom, and willingly exposed herself to public scrutiny because she believed that her story would move the cause of abolition forward.[11] Ida B. Wells was an accomplished journalist who was not afraid to challenge the practice of lynching, which had been justified by false claims that black men were a threat to the presumed purity of white womanhood.[12] The representational strategies that these African American female activists left behind provide us with important narratives about being black, female, and powerful within hostile and oppressive contexts that demanded strategic and aggressive activism to achieve freedom. The written and visual documentation of the

8 contributions of these foremothers has inspired young African American women to pay homage to their legacies and carry on a tradition of using representation to confront stereotypes about black people, as part of larger struggles for social justice.[13]

Popular representations of revolutionary foremothers, such as Ida B. Wells and Sojourner Truth, are associated with their fights to end the enslavement and lynching of black people, and their public images were crafted to create a narrative about African American women that emphasized their piety and purity in the face of dominant narratives that presented black people as oversexed animals who deserved the brutality that they faced in slavery and during reconstruction. Despite the fact that public speaking was seen as inappropriate for "upstanding" women and discouraged by many in the black community, these women continued to not only publically voice their opposition to racism and sexism but also use visual images of themselves as a way to provide messages about black womanhood that were essential to the progress of the race. Dealing with numerous messages within our society that associated black women with loose sexual morals and depravity,[14] these women relied on portraits to project an image of black womanhood that emphasized piety and purity, characteristics that were exclusively attributed to white women.[15]

For example, photographs of famous abolitionist Sojourner Truth played an important role in her work to uplift the race and to counter existing discourses about the immorality of black women. Truth fashioned herself as a respectable, middle-class lady in order to prove her humanity to whites. She was also concerned with the consumption of her image by other blacks.[16] The postcard featuring a portrait of Truth below illustrates the ways that she carefully constructed her visual image to make her campaign for abolition less threatening.

Truth's image is one of a cultured, black lady. The staging of the portrait emphasizes a domestic setting where Truth embodies the image of a modest middle-class woman who sits and knits in her home. Her head, arms, and legs are covered, and her shirt is fully buttoned. This image challenges the image of black women as animalistic, hypersexual, and uncultured savages who were suitable only for menial labor and breeding. It also contrasts with the reality of enslaved African women, who were stripped bare, their bodies exposed to be prodded and sold on the auction block. Truth sits with her knitting, the perfect construction of feminine piety and domesticity, and embraces a middle-class construction of womanhood that directly challenges the relegation of black women outside of that construction.[17]

Remarkably, the caption below this image of Truth (figure 1.1), which reads "I Sell the Shadow to Support the Substance," clearly shows that Truth understood what was at stake and what she needed to do to achieve her goal. Not unlike Michelle Obama, Truth knew that carefully constructing an image that

FIGURE 1.1
Postcard of Sojourner Truth
(ca. 1864)

I Sell the Shadow to Support the Substance.
SOJOURNER TRUTH.

10 countered stereotypes about black women was an important part of what she had to do to support the campaign to end slavery.[18] The resulting image is merely a shadow and can represent only a hint of the reality that was Sojourner Truth and her life.

A shadow is cast when light is placed on an object—the light of public scrutiny that black women face when they dare to speak truth to power. Strong black women seeking social justice must negotiate the negative images of black womanhood while simultaneously crafting an image that will counter the numerous stereotypes that have become a staple part of American popular culture. Selling "the shadow" is one of the strategies that African American women have learned to use to make sure that "the substance" of who they are, the struggles that they face, and the good they desire are not obscured by the insidious narratives and images of black people that support racism, sexism, and other forms of oppression. "Selling the shadow" is what Michelle Obama had to do, and did, during her interview with Larry King. She did so to win the substance of justice.

Both Truth and Obama continued a tradition of speaking truth to power despite the risks. Both knew that in order to be successful advocates they had to face attacks and misrepresentations of African American women. Truth fought for abolition, and Mrs. Obama redirected King's attention on the pressing issues that were the focus of her husband's campaign for president. Truth embodied the dominant ideal of middle-class womanhood in her portrait; Mrs. Obama maintained her composure as she moved the conversation away from the red herring of the angry black woman and refocused King's attention on the important substantive issues facing all Americans. Both managed the negative stereotypes of African American women as part of their work as revolutionary black women.

"Revolutionary black women" refers to African American women who are engaged in progressive or revolutionary politics designed to achieve social justice. This work for justice can involve a number of activities including but not limited to political organizing, writing, performing, and public speaking. Through case studies of revolutionary black women, *Iconic* traces the numerous ways that African American women activists, filmmakers, spectators, writers, and musicians use their versions of the iconic revolutionary black woman to resist oppression and redefine black womanhood. In keeping with feminist analyses of the complex relationship between images and their social contexts, *Iconic* examines images of revolutionary black women and their relationship to sociopolitical movements as well as the ways that visual and narrative culture articulates cultural anxieties about the power of strong African American women. *Iconic* provides a critical way to understand the visual and narrative construction of black revolutionary womanhood across a variety of media texts, such as photography, film, literature, and music. *Iconic* shows how negative stereotypes about the strong, revolutionary black woman are easily deployed to silence and marginalize even the most powerful African American woman in our country, Michelle Obama. From images of activists struggling against racism and sexism in the seventies to musicians who use their music to raise revolutionary consciousness, this study explores the ways that African American women navigate the minefield of stereotypes that permeate American society and construct empowering images of black womanhood that facilitate and support revolutionary change and social justice.

Media outlets in America have consistently relied on outmoded, outdated, negative cultural archetypes to depict and control strong black women because such women produce fear due to the power they exude. The strong revolutionary black woman must negotiate her self-image and identity with the imagistic programming and expectations of various groups, including the African American community and a wider American public that has been fed stereotypical images.[19] Such images cast black women in the roles of the emasculating superwoman/conspirator, the nurturing helpmate, the sexual object, the mammy, and the angry black woman, to name a few.[20] Revolutionary black

12   women know these images well and continue to use strategies of resistance that allow them to assert greater truths about themselves and their experiences as part of a larger struggle against social injustice. Strong black revolutionary women have not allowed negative images to control their life trajectories or their identities. Instead, they engage in a process of point–counterpoint, whereby the stereotypical images sent are strategically assimilated and redefined in order to achieve a pragmatic goal. They refuse to be victimized, though they may utilize modified versions of these negative images, such as accenting physical beauty, clothes, and fashion and reinforcing normative roles and expectations. Michelle Obama patiently tolerated Larry King's persistent questioning and subverted his attempts to depict her as an angry black woman and replaced these attempts with her own agenda by emphasizing her role as mother, wife, and nurturer of the nation. While holding fast to their outspoken commitments to speaking out against police brutality and the prison industrial complex, Kathleen Cleaver and Angela Davis negotiated images of themselves and narratives in the media that relied on stereotypical images of black women that moved between the stereotypical emasculating superwoman/conspirator and the sex object. Societal fears and anxiety provoked by Cleaver, Davis, and other radical activists would be partially ameliorated by Hollywood's image of the sexy, vengeful black woman in blaxploitation films featuring Pam Grier. While Grier managed her self-identity in the face of attempts to conflate her with her on-screen characters, Coffy and Foxy Brown, African American female spectators and directors, such as Etang Inyang, claimed and redefined these stereotypical images as powerful role models of black female power and strength. Black women writers Alice Walker and Audre Lorde crafted complex fictional depictions of African American women and challenged the abuse of black women by black men and the larger society. Despite being depicted as angry black women, Lorde and

Walker served as inspiration for musicians like Erykah Badu and Me'shell Ndegéocello, who confronted stereotypical images of black womanhood while using their music as revolutionary vehicles for social change. *Iconic* decodes images of these revolutionary black women to illustrate how the strong, revolutionary African American woman has pursued societal change through a process of challenging and remaking the negative images imposed on her by a society fearful of her power.

2

REVOLUTIONARY BLACK WOMEN IN THE NEWS

The Politics of Angela Davis and Kathleen Cleaver

Anger. Afro. Avenger. These words capture three characteristics that are often associated with the popular image of the revolutionary black woman. She is angry about injustices that have been committed, and she is not afraid to speak truth to power and to stand with other African Americans in the fight for social justice.[1] Her Afro marks her as one who resists assimilation and instead proudly wears her hair in its natural state as a way to celebrate her African heritage.[2] At her core she is free, and it is this freedom that makes her a threat. There are those who are afraid that she will do what has been done to her and other black people and women—that she will use violence to avenge.[3] In this way she represents blackness and femaleness that cannot be tamed and molded to fit the expectations of whites or blacks who wish her to conform to their standards of behavior. Black women who have come to represent this triple threat emerged because they confronted images created by those who wished to contain their power.

Political activists Angela Davis and Kathleen Cleaver were faced with the stereotypical image of the emasculating super-woman/conspirator promoted by the white media, the tendency of the black media to portray women playing a supportive role

16 in the movement, and the tendency of the media as a whole to treat them as sexual objects. Both negotiated these portrayals as part of their commitment to achieving their revolutionary goals on behalf of the African American community. While the late sixties and early seventies was a period of mass protests, black civil rights groups had a more militant focus. Black civil rights organizations, like the Black Panther Party, advocated black pride, self-help, and self-defense against the police and oppressive governmental forces in the United States.[4] It is within this context that the image of African Americans in the civil rights movement changed. The image of Martin Luther King Jr. linked arm and arm with blacks, whites, and others committed to the achievement of civil rights for all was replaced by the image of young black men, like Huey P. Newton.[5] Images of young African American men in black berets, wielding guns, calling for black self-help and resistance to government oppression and repression circulated in the media. Like the civil rights organizations before them, the emerging black nationalist organizations relied heavily on the participation and support of African American women. The modern feminist movement was also gaining momentum during this time and soon claimed its place as another social justice movement that deployed more militant tactics that contrasted with the more liberal tactics used by many of their contemporaries.[6] African American women who were active and committed to both movements engaged in a sustained critique of the ways that their unique experiences as African American women were obscured by a lack of understanding about the intersecting oppressions based on race, class, and gender.[7]

As an active member of the communist party and for a short time the Black Panther Party, Angela Davis would become one of the most important black female revolutionary activists in the twentieth century.[8] She had passionately expressed her justifiable anger about the treatment of imprisoned African Americans, more specifically the Soledad Brothers, a group of men who had been charged with the death of a prison guard at Soledad Prison.[9] As a university instructor, she not only drew the attention of others who were excited about the growing movements for civil rights in this country but also drew the attention of Ronald Reagan and the California Board of Regents, which ultimately led to her dismissal from her position at UCLA.[10] Her commitment to prison reform and her decision to become active in the case of the Soledad Brothers would eventually lead to her being falsely charged with conspiracy to commit murder and kidnapping. Her flight from the authorities, the FBI manhunt that ultimately led to her capture, imprisonment, and trial, made Angela Davis notorious.[11] Because of the notoriety of her case and the resulting free Angela Davis movement, Davis became an iconic figure in popular culture during the seventies. Images of Davis and the coverage of her case by the white and black media of the time reveal social anxieties about race, gender, sex, and the public role and power of African American women in movements for social justice.

One of the most infamous pictures of Davis is her FBI most wanted poster, which was released in 1970 and circulated nationally and internationally (figure 2.1). The poster contains two shots of Davis side by side. In both photos, she proudly wears her iconic Afro. While the poster lists her age, height, weight, build, hair color, occupation, scars, eyes, complexion, race, and nationality, the Afro in these pictures would become a major character in the unfolding drama that was her life from 1970 to 1972. In the photograph on the left, Davis stares blankly at the camera. In the photo on the right, she has a slight grin. Both pictures suggest a kind of nonchalant indifference that works to construct Davis not as an upstanding citizen and college professor but instead as a cold, calculating killer. The photograph on the left was taken in 1969 and the one on the right was taken in 1970, the year Davis became a fugitive. These dated photographs beg to be read as a story that tells how a beautiful, educated, middle-class, upstanding African American citizen becomes a fugitive. In the "before" shot on the left, Davis' posture is that of a perfect young woman who has been properly taught. In the photo on the right, she slouches. On the left, she wears an unremarkably average scoop neck shirt, unlike the patterned shirt on the right, which appears to be a dashiki, common attire for blacks who embraced their African heritage proudly. In the 1970 shot, she wears dark glasses and has a mischievous, cool smirk on her face, whereas in the 1969 shot she exudes a kind of vulnerability, even as she maintains a stony stare. Reading the two photos featured in the FBI most wanted poster as a linear tale about a good black girl gone bad reveals a deep cultural anxiety about what exists between these two versions of Davis. What stands between any black woman from becoming white America's worst nightmare? The anxiety and concern with answering this question are reflected in the coverage of Davis' story by the white media.

The September 11, 1970, issue of *Life* features a close-up head shot of Davis with her head slightly bowed (figure 2.3).[12] The unflattering black-and-white photograph covers the entire page and emphasizes the dark circles under Davis' eyes. The headline, "The Making of a Fugitive," is positioned within her large Afro and draws attention to her head and by extension her mind. She appears to be in deep thought, and one wonders what she is thinking.

The feature article, "The Path of Angela Davis," juxtaposes a photo of Davis in grade school with her FBI most wanted poster.[13] The article begins, "The generous schoolgirl mouth smiles with the soft and steady eyes."[14] A description of the young Davis' "generous schoolgirl mouth" and her "steady eyes" has sexual connotations and seems inappropriate. This sentence is immediately followed by a discussion of how Davis' mother remembers Davis being "a happy, average, loving child."[15] Describing the young Davis' eyes and mouth does nothing to support the overall purpose of an article that seeks to explore how this average middle-class girl became a radical revolutionary. In fact, the photograph of "the remarkable Davis family" and the picture of her first graduation on the following page seem much more illustrative of Davis' upbringing and early childhood.[16] While the article gives a thorough account of Davis' path to becoming a fugitive that emphasizes her intellect and academic accomplishments, there are moments in the article that seem irrelevant to the overall purpose of the piece. For example, the article includes a quote from a friend that discusses how "men followed her down Paris streets and stumbled over each other to light her cigarettes."[17] This quote is in the section of the article titled "Relentless Honing of a Brilliant Mind" but adds nothing to our understanding of Davis' brilliance—but everything to her construction as a sexualized object. The compulsion to return to Davis' physical attributes (eyes, mouth, and hair) shows how sexual objectification is used to harness her power as a black woman.

Like other accounts of Davis' activism in both the white and the black press, the exposé includes a photograph of Davis with her mouth wide open speaking into a microphone at a rally. The section titled "A Brilliant Scholar Shifts toward Perilous Commitment" tries to reconcile Davis the brilliant and accomplished professor with Davis the angry, unspoken activist who was on the run. According to one of her male colleagues,

> Angela had the best education the white Western world can give anyone.... She didn't reject any of it. I have been asked what she was reading, what influenced her to make this change from studious, quiet, intellectual pursuits to what some people want to call "rabid revolutionary." She was just walking around this country with her eyes open. People seem to want to believe that some great change had come over her. "Did she suddenly speak more violently?" they ask. "Did her Afro suddenly grow out higher and wider?" "Was she suddenly fanatic and nervous?" It's simply not true—none of that. The only thing I noticed is that toward the end of the summer she was very tired.[18]

This quote poignantly illustrates the anxiety that is created when a seemingly well-adjusted African American professional is outspoken, explicit, and unapologetic about her critiques of the status quo. The speaker's humorous reference to the size of

ANTED# ICONIC

20

WANTED BY THE FBI

INTERSTATE FLIGHT - MURDER, KIDNAPING
ANGELA YVONNE DAVIS

FBI No. 867,615 G

Photograph taken 1969   Photograph taken 1970

Alias: "Tamu"

DESCRIPTION

Age:	26, born January 26, 1944, Birmingham, Alabama		
Height:	5'8"	Eyes:	Brown
Weight:	145 pounds	Complexion:	Light brown
Build:	Slender	Race:	Negro
Hair:	Black	Nationality:	American
Occupation:	Teacher		
Scars and Marks:	Small scars on both knees		

Fingerprint Classification: 4 M 5 Ua 6
                             I 17 U

CAUTION

ANGELA DAVIS IS WANTED ON KIDNAPING AND MURDER CHARGES GROWING OUT OF AN ABDUCTION AND SHOOTING IN MARIN COUNTY, CALIFORNIA, ON AUGUST 7, 1970. SHE ALLEGEDLY HAS PURCHASED SEVERAL GUNS IN THE PAST. CONSIDER POSSIBLY ARMED AND DANGEROUS.

A Federal warrant was issued on August 15, 1970, at San Francisco, California, charging Davis with unlawful interstate flight to avoid prosecution for murder and kidnaping (Title 18, U. S. Code, Section 1073).

IF YOU HAVE ANY INFORMATION CONCERNING THIS PERSON, PLEASE NOTIFY ME OR CONTACT YOUR LOCAL FBI OFFICE. TELEPHONE NUMBERS AND ADDRESSES OF ALL FBI OFFICES LISTED ON BACK.

DIRECTOR
FEDERAL BUREAU OF INVESTIGATION
UNITED STATES DEPARTMENT OF JUSTICE
WASHINGTON, D. C. 20535
TELEPHONE, NATIONAL 8-7117

Entered NCIC
Wanted Flyer 457
August 18, 1970

FIGURE 2.1
FBI Most Wanted Poster of Davis

Davis' Afro is an excellent example of the way that beauty and fashion were read as predictors of one's propensity to engage in radical and/or criminal behavior. The juxtaposition of questions about the size of Davis' Afro and whether she suddenly began to speak violently illustrates the ways that revolutionaries and radical protest are read as irrational. In the mind of the average

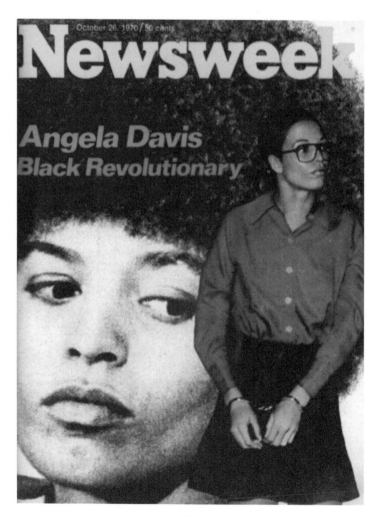

FIGURE 2.2
Cover of Newsweek, *October 26, 1970*

22

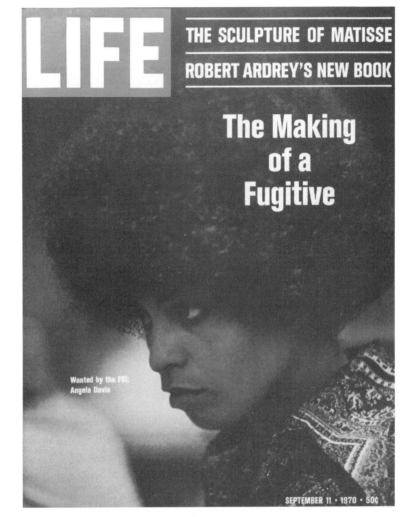

FIGURE 2.3
Angela Davis on the September 11, 1970, Issue of Life

American who has been fed a steady diet of stereotypical images of angry blacks and women, brandishing guns and burning their bras, the shift from upstanding American citizen and outspoken radical activist could never be rational or based on a legitimate critique of the status quo.

While Davis was on the run, she wore numerous disguises that included glasses and wigs with straight hair (figure 2.1). Davis' beauty and the construction of her as a dangerous threat converge in the October 26, 1970, issue of *Newsweek* (figure 2.2).[19] The large black-and-white shot of her head, like the *Life* cover (figure 2.3), focuses attention on her mind. This reminds the reader that Davis' intelligence is the most dangerous threat that she poses and reinforces the stereotype of the emasculating superwoman/conspirator. The construction of black women as masterminds behind the movement is related to the stereotype of the domineering black matriarch who is accused of emasculating black men, causing the destruction of the black family and community.[20] The cover reminds us that Davis is accused of planning an escape attempt that resulted in the death of several people.

In addition to reinforcing the stereotype of black women as matriarchal leaders of the movement, the position of the two contrasting images of Davis on the cover invokes another story about black women and their power, specifically their sexual power. Davis' eyes are downcast, and the photographs are arranged in a way to imply she is admiring her own image. The arrangement of the photos guides the viewer's eye away from Davis' head or mind, shifting attention to her legs and thighs. The depiction of the handcuffed Davis in her sexy disguise functions as a type of containment of the powerful, strong black woman. Consequently, anxieties about the educated black revolutionary woman are assuaged by her sexual objectification.[21]

Like the mainstream white press, the black press covered Davis' case extensively. Justice for Davis became an important goal of the Black Panther Party. The party newspaper featured her on the cover and ran impassioned editorials praising Davis for her work on behalf of the Soledad Brothers and other political prisoners. For example, the November 20, 1971, issue of *The Black Panther* decries the selection of an all-white jury to hear Davis' case (figure 2.4).[22] After Davis was acquitted and released

24

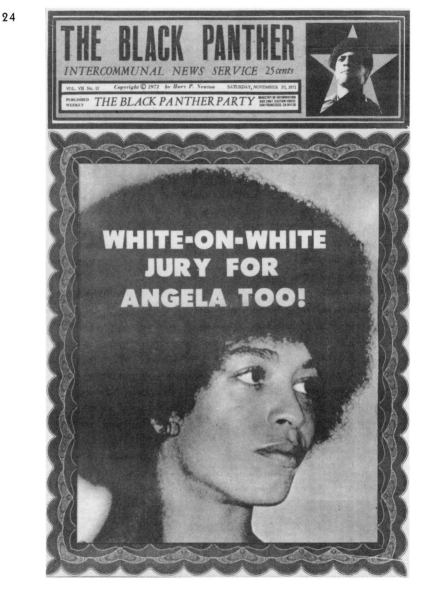

FIGURE 2.4
Davis on the Cover of the November 20, 1971, Issue of The Black Panther

from prison, she continued her work on behalf of prisoners. She **25** also continued her work with the Communist Party. Despite her commitment to radical activism on behalf of blacks and other disenfranchised groups, her involvement with the Black Panther Party was very limited. That group would eventually scold Davis for not remaining active in the Black Panther Party.[23]

Like the cover of *The Black Panther, Jet*'s May 6, 1971, cover featuring Davis celebrates her brains and her beauty. The headline reads "Angela Davis Case Puts Justice on Trial." Cordell S. Thompson's story includes several photos of Davis and emphasizes her role as a symbol of the movement against *racial* oppression. Thompson begins his piece by describing the iconic symbol of justice, the Greek goddess Themis. He explains,

> In her left hand are scales on which the conflicting claims of antagonists are weighed, and she is blindfolded to prevent her from favoring one over the other. In the right hand she holds the double-edged sword of justice, with its tip blunted so that when she brings down the sword on a target it is tempered with mercy.[24]

This statement is followed by a discussion of the quest for justice as it relates to the black man in America. Whereas the Greek goddess stands in as a representation of Western and specifically American ideals of justice, the text positions Angela Davis as an iconic figure of justice for the imprisoned African American male. According to Thompson, "At this stage of the Black man's travail in America, perhaps no one person symbolizes what Blacks consider the injustice done to Blacks in America's legal and judicial system than former UCLA philosophy instructor Angela Davis, in jail awaiting trial in California in connection with the courthouse shootout in San Rafael, Calif., last Aug. 7, in which four persons died, including a judge."[25] Thompson emphasizes that the trial of "the beautiful Miss Davis means many things, but on one thing there is much agreement: that she is a 'political prisoner.'"[26] Thompson goes on to highlight that the black community is supporting Davis because she is black, not because she is a communist. He claims that "Blacks see Communism or

26

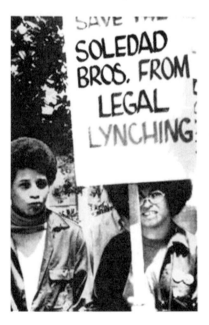

Rapping about racism, Angela Davis holds attention of a Los Angeles rally in October, 1970.

SAVE THE
SOLEDAD
BROS. FROM
LEGAL
LYNCHING

A REVEALING REPORT

BY ROBERT A. DeLEON
Jet Managing Editor

The land is lush with sun-ripened foliage and roads winding through the hills of what some might say is California's most beautiful countryside. Most of its residents are affluent and would be looked upon as unlikely hosts for one of the most historic proceedings in the country's history.

And yet, sitting atop a low range of hills is the Marin County Civic Center and, in one of its two cigar-shaped corridors, called the Hall of Justice, is housed Angela Yvonne Davis.

Miss Davis, a former University of California professor, has been charged with murder, kidnaping and conspiracy in connection with the August 7, 1970, shootout at the center which resulted in the death of four persons, including Jonathan Peter Jackson, 17-year-old brother of the recently killed George (Soledad Brother) Jackson, and a judge, Harold J. Haley. Most of Miss Davis' time, since her imprisonment a year ago, has been spent in a two-room cell containing a work room and a sleeping room, but the most important periods of her life these days are spent in a place called Courtroom Number 3. It is one of four such rooms along the corridor, all of which, in their own right, will be remembered in history.

In Courtroom Number 1, six in-

Protesting on behalf of Black inmates at Soledad prison, Miss Davis joins Jonathan Jackson, who was killed two months later.

FIGURE 2.5

ON ANGELA DAVIS' FIGHT FOR FREEDOM

Sprawling Marin County Civic Center is where Angela is confined until she is transferred to stand trial. Jonathan, brother of slain George Jackson, was killed in shootout at the modern facility in August, 1970.

mates from San Quentin prison, who are said to have been involved in the alleged escape attempt of George Jackson, are being tried. Courtroom Number 2 has been used little since that day last year when Jonathan Jackson and four inmates allegedly kidnaped a judge and several jurors involved in a case there. And then, there is Courtroom Number 4 which remains boarded from floor to ceiling as the result of a mysterious explosion last year that has not yet been explained.

Persons desiring entrance to Courtroom Number 3 receive a thorough search outside Courtroom Number 4 and, having entered the room where hearings into Miss Davis' case are held, find that all exits are locked and guarded by armed sheriff's deputies.

At this point, assistant California Atty. Gen. Albert Harris Jr., who is prosecuting the case, doesn't have much to say in the hearings held before Judge Richard E. Arnason, the sixth judge involved in the case. But Miss Davis and her attorneys, headed by Howard Moore of Atlanta, Ga., almost constantly offer motions in the carpeted room calling for a variety of considerations they feel are necessary to ensure a fair trial.

The 27-year-old Miss Davis, sitting between Moore and co-counsel Margaret Burnham at a semi-circular table, often addresses the court herself, but never with the emotion that has been witnessed at the trials of other radicals, prompting one observer to note, "For all the life of her, she seems

Angela Davis in the November 18, 1971, Issue of Jet

28   Marxism as only offering Blacks a philosophy that deters from nation building."[27] This discussion of Davis unwittingly privileges the experience of the black male revolutionary because it positions Davis' struggle as secondary to the overall struggle of male political prisoners, despite the fact that black women were also imprisoned as part of the concerted campaign to crush black nationalist movements.[28]

Later in Thompson's article, he focuses on the grieving mother of Jonathan Jackson, the younger brother of prisoner George Jackson, who allegedly took orders from Davis as part of his attempt to free his brother in the infamous courthouse shootout. Mrs. Jackson makes it clear that her son would never take orders from a woman. The caption for the story reads, "Mother Says Son Was a Man, Needed No Woman's Advice."[29] She says, "I knew my son better than anybody, and I know that he wouldn't let anybody tell him what to do unless he wanted to do it himself, and I know he wouldn't let any woman tell him what to do. That I know."[30] By reprinting this quote, Thompson uses the strength of black masculinity as proof of Angela Davis' innocence. In other words, no real black man—which Jonathan presumably was—would have taken orders from a woman. Therefore, Davis could not possibly be considered the mastermind of a conspiracy to free the Soledad Brothers from prison.

Jet's November 18, 1971, issue, "A Revealing Report on Angela Davis' Fight for Freedom," shows Angela Davis on the cover seated at a table in the courtroom.[31] She looks serious and sad as she contemplates the case against her. The table is covered with files and legal books presumably being used by the defense. The opening of Robert DeLeon's article features a picture of Davis with her mouth open, as she speaks out at a Los Angeles rally in 1970 (figure 2.5).[32] Like the earlier examples, the picture with her mouth open reinforces the angry black woman stereotype. However, this stereotype is mitigated by the fact that the article praises Davis for her outspoken activism. Below this picture is another famous photograph of Davis standing next to Jonathan Jackson at a protest calling for the release of the Soledad Brothers.[33] In addition, there is short section with a caption that reads "Moore Assails Use of Unopened Letters in the Trial," which includes a brief discussion of the prosecution's use of an unopened letter to George Jackson from Davis in which she declares her love for him, along with some political discussion.[34] The juxtaposition of photos of Davis and Jackson links them as lovers and constructs Davis as a woman who, because she was desperately in love, would do anything to save her lover from prison. Depictions of revolutionary women who sacrifice themselves for the love of a good black man serve a theatrical function.[35] This narrative would be highlighted and further glamorized in Hollywood's fictionalized account of the political activism and love affair between George Jackson and Angela Davis, Brothers, released in 1977, which is discussed later in this chapter.

Another feature on Davis in Jet reinforces Davis' role in the struggle in terms of her activism and sacrifices, while simultaneously emphasizing her image as a symbol of iconic revolutionary beauty. The February 24, 1972, issue features an interview with the incarcerated Davis. The headline reads "A Look at Angela Davis from Another Angle: Her Jail Cell." The cover features Davis with eyes slightly downcast. She appears to be taking a break from speaking. Her hair frames her face as she looks slightly down with her shoulders slightly hunched over. The feature also includes an exclusive photo gallery featuring six photographs of Davis and carrying the caption, "A Gallery of Moods of Angela Davis" (figure 2.6). This title suggests a desire to penetrate the inner world of the activist through the visual. It is not clear from the various shots that there is a definite separation of moods suggested by Davis' various poses. Under the title there is a paragraph that reads, "The many months of life behind bars have taken their toll. Despite it all, Angela Davis maintains a kind of beauty and can still manage an occasional smile."[36]

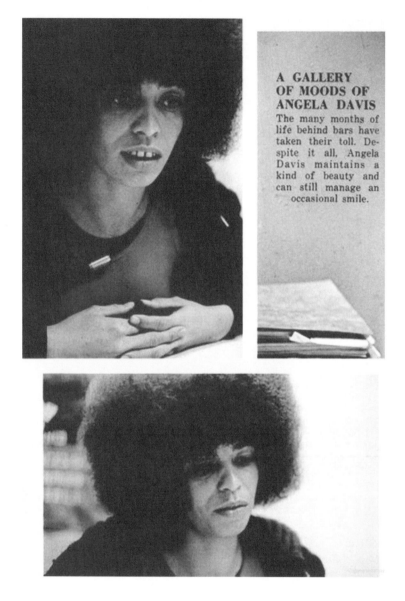

A GALLERY
OF MOODS OF
ANGELA DAVIS
The many months of life behind bars have taken their toll. Despite it all, Angela Davis maintains a kind of beauty and can still manage an occasional smile.

FIGURE 2.6

Angela Davis in the February 24, 1972, Issue of Jet

Miss Davis cautions that efforts should be undertaken to free all political prisoners.

During pre-trial session, Angela talks with her sister, Fania, as pickets (below) march outside courtroom.

Speaks About King

ther Party and a couple of other very aggressive kinds of issues means something with respect to the entire movement. I think it's very important to always have people within the system, always prodding the system, always calling, pointing out, exposing it."

Speaking of the late Rev. Martin L. King Jr., Miss Davis noted that "at the time he was assassinated, (he) was headed in a very radical direction." In some of his final speeches, she said, "he said some very interesting, radical things about the urban rebellion. He talked about the need to bring the struggle for Black liberation to the global struggle against imperialism. He talked about socialism."

Addressing herself to the recent split between Rev. Ralph Abernathy, president of the Southern Christian Leadership Conference (SCLC), and Rev. Jesse Jackson, which resulted in the formation of Operation PUSH (People United to Save Humanity), Miss Davis said, "It's just too bad that people were not prepared for it.

"I feel that Rev. Abernathy is attempting to develop and extend what Martin Luther King was beginning to develop at the time he was assassinated. Jesse Jackson, on the other hand, is moving in the direction of Black capitalism. I believe that a lot of people are following Jesse Jackson who really don't understand what's been going on and what that means.

"Rev. Abernathy has taken, I think, the most consistent position

FIGURE 2.6

on political prisoners of any group or organization of that character in this country. . . . Jesse Jackson represents the old and traditional, except (his conversation) just has a little militant rhetoric to it."

Attorneys for Miss Davis, headed by Howard Moore, of Atlanta, Ga., are now arguing last-minute motions before her trial, which is expected to begin some time next month. Miss Davis has been granted permission to act as co-counsel in the presentation of her defense and, during the interview, said that she will personally handle those questions raised during the proceedings which concern her political beliefs.

"The prosecutor, in developing his own case," she said, "has shown us already . . . that my political activities are going to be at stake. I feel that when it is a question of my political beliefs and political activities, I can most effectively deal with this since I can most effectively counter the charges against me when they are political in character."

Miss Davis and her attorneys have said they feel it is impossible for her to receive a fair trial in Santa Clara County and Miss Davis said if it is decided that she is innocent, "it will be a people's victory. Just as the fact that Huey (Newton) and Ericka (Huggins) and Bobby (Seale) and the New York 21 (Black Panthers) were released. Those were people's victories.

"That was not what liberal circles wanted to call it, namely, the fairness and justice that's inher-

Miss Davis, wearing heavy sweater and boots, stands near flag sent by Black prisoners in Korea.

ent in the system itself. Because, if there had been fairness and justice inherent in the system itself, they would never have been brought to trial."

If she is found innocent of the charges pressed against her, Miss Davis says she will devote all of her time to "communicate more concretely to people on the outside what it means to be in one of these monstrous maximum security prisons in America.

"The people have to understand what the forces were that drove

(CONT.)

DeLeon focuses on Davis' beauty and laments the ways that the almost two-year imprisonment caused Davis to age.[37] Despite this initial fixation on Davis' physical beauty, DeLeon eventually shifts his focus from Davis' "physical characteristics [which] have seldom gone unnoticed" to her intelligence and her many intellectual accomplishments.[38] Another picture in the exclusive interview shows Davis standing in front of a flag that was sent to her by black prisoners in Korea (figure 2.6). The caption for this photograph focuses more on Davis' fashion than the political implications for black international solidarity that the gift evokes. The caption reads, "Miss Davis, wearing heavy sweater and boots, stands near flag sent by Black prisoners in Korea."[39] This statement privileges her physical beauty over other aspects of her political persona and the racial solidarity that the gift evokes. DeLeon's interview illustrates the familiar trope of black women as nurturing helpmates and sacrificial lambs for the struggle. Davis reinforces this narrative by not focusing on her own suffering, instead cautioning the readers not to focus on her alone. She reminds readers that there are "many brothers who are much worse off than [she is]."[40] This statement is a perfect example of how the rhetoric used by men and women in black revolutionary movements often focused on the ways that racist oppression hurt black men and, by extension, the entire black community, instead of illustrating the specificity of black women's oppression. It also shows the ways that Davis reinforced the image of black women as nurturing helpmates in the movement.[41]

Pictures of Davis after her release from prison also shed light on how images of black revolutionary icons function as part of a wider discourse about African American women in the struggle. The May 16, 1974, issue of *Jet* includes a follow-up story by Robert A. DeLeon about the work for prison reform that consumed most of Davis' time after her release. In her discussion with DeLeon, Davis comments on her depiction in the mainstream media:

> The problem is that before and during the trial, the white press projected an image of a raving militant talking about burning and violence; there were pictures of me with my mouth wide open all

of the time. Well, now they are finding trouble justifying that image through the work we're doing so they just don't cover the activities of our organization.[42]

In this article, which chronicles Davis' activities to increase awareness about political repression, there is still considerable interest in her personal and romantic life. The last paragraph of the article includes questions about Davis' dating life. She responds,

> And if that's what you're all about, there's not much time left for other things. You know, . . . I've been out on a date maybe twice—two times—since I was acquitted. And I like to party, I like to go to the movies but I just haven't been able to do it because the other things are just so much more important.[43]

While this statement clearly shows Davis' priorities, the line of questioning reveals an anxiety about the availability of Davis as a sexual object of black male desire. The conversation between Davis and DeLeon reveals that the focus on heterosexual relationships between black men and women is used to portray an undivided front for the movement.

For members of the Black Panther Party, images of black women wielding handguns while carrying babies on their backs were used to put those who would attack the black community on notice that black women were armed and ready to defend themselves. The Black Panther Party used images of women as well as other visual images and the media to raise consciousness and to project a representation of black people and masculinity that was threatening to white Americans.[44] In addition, the images and rhetoric of the movement privileged the experiences of black men and strongly encouraged black women to choose the black power movement instead of the growing feminist movement of the period. Kathleen Cleaver has experienced this enforced split and tension between revolutionary activism and feminism. She explains,

> At times, during the question and answer session following a speech I'd given, someone would ask, "What is the woman's role in the Black

Panther Party?" I never liked that question. I'd give a short answer: "It's the same as men." We are revolutionaries, I'd explain. Back then, I didn't understand why they wanted to think of what men were doing and what women were doing as separate. It's taken me years, literally about 25 years, to understand that what I really didn't like was the underlying assumption motivating the question. The assumption held that being part of a revolutionary movement was in conflict with what the questioner had been socialized to believe was appropriate conduct for a woman. That convoluted concept never entered my head, although I am certain it was far more widely accepted than I ever realized.[45]

Within the Black Panther Party, sex and women's bodies were seen as commodities to be exchanged in service of the revolution.[46] This is apparent in the representations of revolutionary black women such as Kathleen Cleaver. The photograph of Cleaver on the facing page (figure 2.7) is a clear example of the ways that representations of black female revolutionaries functioned as part of a campaign to promote fear and trepidation. Another black-and-white photograph from that period is very similar, featuring Cleaver dressed entirely in black, wearing an Afro and sunglasses. She is grasping a gun in her right hand, while she poses with her left hand on her hip. She looks directly into the camera with a slight smirk. This photograph combines feminine allure with the phallic symbol of the gun to directly challenge white police violence and position black women as potential threats to the racist status quo. While the image is a part of a common practice during the sixties and seventies of posing feminine women with guns,[47] it is further complicated by the way that it links black female strength with traditional ideas about the role of women in the home, as well as in the movement. The photograph marks Cleaver as a threat not only because she has a gun but also because of her marital relationship with Eldridge Cleaver, one of the leaders of the Black Panther Party. This image was a "tactical and symbolic challenge to police raids on the apartment that she shared with Eldridge Cleaver, who as an ex-convict could not legally possess weapons.

FIGURE 2.7
*Kathleen Cleaver in the September 13, 1969,
Issue of* The Black Panther

KATHLEEN

According to Cleaver, soon after the photo was taken, she left the country and had no control over the use of the image."[48] The image also appeared on a cover of the Black Panther Party newspaper and later circulated as a poster. Her short skirt and pose emphasize her femininity and sexuality, while her leaning on the gun suggests that she has the confidence and ability to use it if needed. While the gun clearly stands as a warning to potential intruders, the slight grin on her face and her stance at the door are reminiscent of a wife welcoming guests into her home. The photograph of Cleaver casts her in the role of the dutiful wife and mediator between home as a sanctuary for the male revolutionary and the liberation struggle that is raging beyond its boundaries. In this way, Cleaver becomes the queen of the Black Panther Party, who reigns alongside her revolutionary king.

The depiction of the ideal black revolutionary family is illustrated by a photo from the August 16, 1969, cover of *The Black*

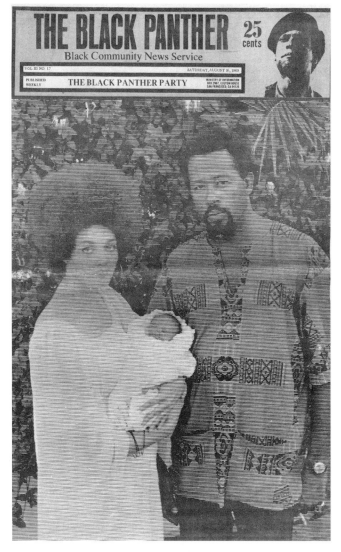

FIGURE 2.8
Kathleen and Eldridge Cleaver on the Cover of the August 16, 1969,
Issue of The Black Panther

Panther (figure 2.8). Kathleen Cleaver holds her newborn son, posing with her husband. The feature article announcing Antonio Maceo Cleaver begins with the line, "A new revolutionary warrior has been born in our midst" and goes on to discuss how the newborn was named after Antonio Maceo, founder of the Cuban Revolutionary Party who led an uprising against Spain in 1895.[49] This image of a thriving black revolutionary family reinforces the emphasis on traditional gender roles within the discourse of the organization. The reference to Antonio as a revolutionary warrior links the bearing of children to the revolutionary struggle, urging other revolutionaries to birth children who will eventually fight for the goals of the organization. This photograph supports the prevailing belief that having and raising revolutionary children was an important role that black women were to play in the movement.

Cleaver's dual role as wife and liberator is reflected in the following covers from *Jet*. The cover of the February 26, 1970, issue announces her acting debut in Michelangelo Antonioni's film *Zabriskie Point* (1970) and defines her as the "outspoken wife of self-exiled Black Panther leader" (figure 2.9). The emphasis on her status as panther wife is less prominent in the December 2, 1971, issue which heralds the return of Cleaver, "the Black liberator" (figure 2.10). The earlier cover appears to be a picture that was taken of Cleaver while she was giving a speech, whereas the later photograph appears to have been posed specifically for the cover. Despite its emphasis on Cleaver's action as a liberator, the photograph of Cleaver with a closed mouth deemphasizes her role as activist and instead highlights her construction as a representation of the movement. In fact, the absence of a background associated with activism, such as a protest or a gathering of other activists, further emphasizes her function as an image rather than as a leader and vital part of the black revolutionary struggle.

Cleaver's function as a symbol of the movement is poignantly illustrated in her cameo role in *Zabriskie Point*, Antonioni's 1970 film about radical youth protests during the sixties in America. Antonioni's decision to use actual members of the Black Panther Party added authenticity to the film.[50] The opening scene takes

FIGURE 2.9
Cleaver on the Cover of the February 26, 1970, Issue of Jet

place in an auditorium on a college campus, where students are planning an unspecified protest. However, there are specific references to the struggle of black people against police brutality. Kathleen Cleaver is seated at the front table facing the audience.

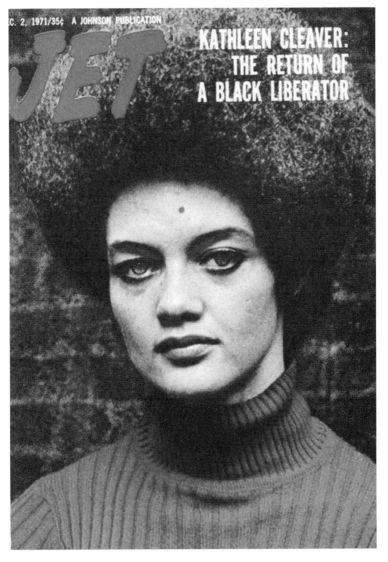

FIGURE 2.10
Cleaver on the Cover of the December 2, 1971, Issue of Jet

Her black male comrade talks confidently as she listens intently for most of this opening scene, making just one statement. Antonioni uses close-up shots that focus on the various individuals in the room, including Cleaver, who, positioned at the center of

42   the table surrounded by other activists, serves as the focal point in the scene. She is visually central in this depiction of revolutionary student struggle, while simultaneously remaining relatively silent when compared to the other people in the scene. This further illustrates how black female revolutionaries were often used as showpieces for the movement, primarily present to be seen, not heard. Despite the fact that these women were quite outspoken and active in the daily activities of radical organizations, their visual representations reinforced their roles as nurturing helpmates to black men in movement.

Brothers was written by Edward and Mildred Lewis and directed by Arthur Barron. The film is a fictionalized account of the incarceration of George Jackson and his relationship with Angela Davis. The film primarily focuses on the injustices faced by David Thomas, an inmate who is unfairly imprisoned and develops a relationship with the revolutionary professor Paula Jones. The main character, David Thomas (representing Jackson), is played by football player and blaxploitation star Bernie Casey. Professor Paula Jones (representing Davis) is played by Vonetta McGee, another well-known blaxploitation actress. Some critics of the film were disappointed with the selection of these actors to represent such important black revolutionary activists. In a review in the April 18, 1977, issue of *Time*, Christopher Porterfield proclaims a generally negative view of the film. What is most striking about his review is his critique of the performance of Vonetta McGee. He is particularly concerned with the ways that the Paula Jones character played by McGee "drifts in and out with all the serenity of a model in a soap commercial and with none of the biting intellectuality of Angela Davis."[51] Porterfield is correct that overall Professor Jones' beauty and grace are far more emphasized than her intellectual prowess. For example, in a critical scene that depicts the meeting of the main characters, the dialogue and camera are used to glamorize Professor Jones. As Professor Jones and a senator tour the prison with the warden, David and his cellmates use a mirror to watch Professor Jones saunter down the cellblock. Romantic calypso music, which would later become the couple's theme, plays in the background as David projects Paula's image through a tiny mirror. He leans over to his cellmate, played by Ron O'Neal, another well-known blaxploitation actor, and says that Jones is "a real foxy lady." As she approaches his cell, David says, "Hey Professor Jones." Paula responds, "Hey brother." He then continues to explain how he has been admiring her picture on the cover of her book and that he has learned a great deal from her writing. While it is clear that David acknowledges Professor Jones' intellect, the dialogue in this scene clearly privileges her attractiveness. This happens in the scene when David tries to capture Davis in the mirror as she walks through the prison and when he comments about admiring her picture before he mentions her work.

As the film continues, Professor Jones realizes that David is the brother of Joshua, a young high school student who seeks her help in exposing the injustices of the prison system in California. They begin corresponding via letters, and eventually she visits him to conduct an interview. David is shackled, and Paula is reprimanded by the guard when she attempts to touch his hands across the table. This is the extent of their physical contact, but the sexual tension between the couple is heightened by the calypso music playing in the background during their visit. Shortly after this scene, Thomas tells one of his fellow inmates that "Sister Jones gave [him] a jones."[52] This dialogue illustrates the persistent fascination with Davis' beauty and her availability to black men as a sexual object, reminiscent of the objectification of black women that had become a defining feature of blaxploitation films.

Despite the plethora of famous blaxploitation actors in the film, the writers of Brothers claim that the film should not be considered an exploitation film, like other black-themed urban movies produced at the time.[53] John Cocchi's interview with the writers claims that the letters that were used in the film were

44   the actual letters that George Jackson and Angela Davis sent to each other and that "Davis liked [the] film."[54] Whether or not these claims are true, it is evident that the objectification and representation of black female revolutionaries like Davis and Cleaver as sex objects, nurturing helpmates, and emasculating superwomen who conspire to overthrow the government reveals societal anxieties about their power as agitators for revolutionary change. The media focus on sexuality and physical appearance functioned as a way for whites and blacks to work through cultural anxieties about the power and appropriate role of black women in radical, revolutionary movements during the seventies. The resulting images fueled the exaggerated representations of sexy, violent, and angry black women in film.

3

REVOLUTIONARY BLACK WOMEN IN FILM
Blaxploitation and the Legacy of Pam Grier

Stereotypical images of revolutionary black women became more accessible through the characters in blaxploitation films. The black female heroine in blaxploitation films served as a way to make "real" revolutionary women more palatable to the masses. Just as the sexual objectification of Angela Davis served to contain the threat that she posed as a strong, powerful revolutionary activist, blaxploitation films reinforced the stereotype of the dangerous and angry black woman while simultaneously recuperating her through a process of sexual objectification that worked to mitigate the fear and anxiety that she caused. Blaxploitation films relied on a cool and aloof protagonist, an urban setting, violence, sexual encounters with black and white women, white villains, superficial acknowledgment of the problems of lower-class blacks, and a throbbing musical score.[1] These low-budget Hollywood films were primarily designed to shock and titillate audiences by glamorizing urban culture and elevating the "pimp/outlaw/rebel [to the status of] folk hero."[2] Early blaxploitation films relegated black women to minor roles that supported the male protagonists, not unlike the ways that real women in the movement were relegated to the roles of nurturing

46 helpmates. The popularity of the genre has been attributed to the success of Melvin Van Peeble's famous independent film, *Sweet Sweetback's Baadasssss Song* (1971), which piqued Hollywood's interest in attracting a black audience.[3] Unfortunately, many of these films reinforced stereotypes about black people.[4] After the initial success of blaxploitation films featuring male leads, Hollywood began featuring black female heroines in films such as *Cleopatra Jones* (Jack Starrett, 1973), *Get Christie Love!* (William A. Graham, 1974), and *TNT Jackson* (Cirio Santiago, 1974).[5] In many of these films, the women were gorgeous sex objects contained within an inner-city environment characterized by violence, crime, and drug abuse. These women were not victims of their environment—they were superwomen who fought white and black criminals, using femininity and sex to lure and eventually destroy their prey.[6] Blaxploitation films affirmed the perception that black women were invulnerable, stronger than white women, and the physical equal of any man of their race.[7] In addition to reinforcing the image of the angry, dangerous, emasculating black woman, the narratives and filming techniques privileged a male perspective that objectified and sexualized African American women.[8] The black female heroine in blaxploitation films reinforced stereotypes about the threat posed by real revolutionary women, while simultaneously creating a space where black women were safely contained in a dangerous inner-city world, where poor white and black people killed each other.[9] This world was far removed from the world of law-abiding middle- and upper-class Americans and served to allay some of the growing anxieties about strong blacks and women who were in the streets protesting as part of the black power and feminist movements.

Pam Grier is the most well-known and celebrated actress of the genre. She began her acting career in low-budget women-in-prison films, which later led to her performing the starring role in *Coffy* (Jack Hill, 1973) and her most famous role as the title character in *Foxy Brown* (Jack Hill, 1974). Grier's performances in these films and large fan base cemented her place as one of the most celebrated African American actresses of the period. Pam Grier's fans were largely black, inner-city, adolescent males.[10] However, the pleasure of watching Grier was not limited to men.[11] Despite the popularity of her films, coordinated efforts by black civil rights groups resulted in waning popularity and profits and ultimately led to the genre's demise. While the decrease in the popularity of blaxploitation films initially had a negative impact on Grier's ability to move beyond the superheroine figure with which she is associated, she has nonetheless maintained a relatively successful career as a television and film star and most recently as a cast member of the cable television drama *The L Word*.[12]

In *Coffy*, Grier plays a lone vigilante who pursues and murders the drug dealer who is responsible for her younger sister's addiction to drugs. Coffy uses her brains, beauty, and connections to find the low-level drug dealer. She also exposes a black councilman who participated in a plot to allow the white kingpin of the drug racket to continue bringing drugs into the community. The movie poster for *Coffy* reveals the ways that Hollywood films featuring black female heroines were used to negotiate anxieties about the increasingly more militant black men and women. Blaxploitation films and the promotional materials used to advertise them, such as posters and press kits, were part of a process of containing black female activists by producing images that depicted sexy and strong black women who were associated with crime, violence, and vigilante justice.

In the promotional poster for *Coffy*, the title character appears in a sexualized manner, her hand on her hip and her facial expression clearly representing a warning similar to that depicted in the photograph of Kathleen Cleaver (figure 3.1). Both images evoke fear of black women with guns and use Afrocentric beauty and femininity to represent African American women.[13] However, the drawing of Grier as Coffy is far more sexualized than the photograph of Cleaver. Coffy's stomach is exposed, and

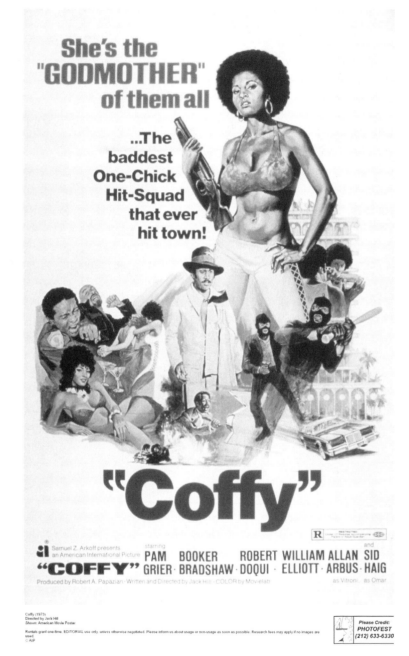

FIGURE 3.1
Promotional Movie Poster for Coffy (1973)

her halter exposes her large bust. Her size in relationship to that of other characters positions her as dominant, looming over the other characters, particularly the black man positioned in front of her thigh and pubic area. This establishes a clear hierarchy where black men are subordinate to black women. Immediately under her right thigh appear images of white men in masks with guns, clearly identifying them as criminals. Her size and her position establish the fact that Coffy is a threat not only to black men but also to white men. Towering over the drawings of fighting blacks and whites, she transcends and claims her position as the "Godmother of them all." Using the term *Godmother* on the poster references the term *Godfather*, which is associated with the mafia and gangster films such as *The Godfather*. More importantly, using the term *Godmother* establishes her as the one with the ultimate control over who dies and lives and reinforces the myth that African American women are calculating masterminds, directing the moves made by black men. In addition to Militant Coffy pictured in the poster, her alter ego Sexy Coffy lounges in a bikini at

FIGURE 3.2
Promotional Photograph for Coffy *(1973)*

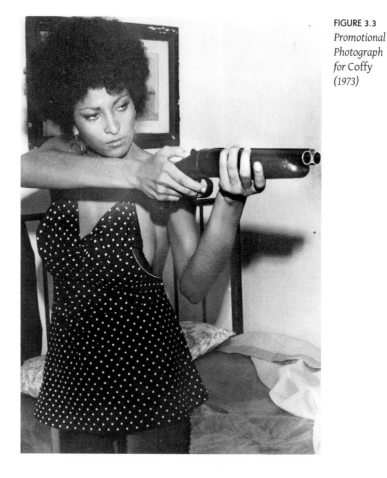

FIGURE 3.3
*Promotional
Photograph
for* Coffy
(1973)

the bottom left of the page, which establishes the sexy version of the lead character as simply a role used to achieve the goals of the Coffy who delivers justice.

Photographs of Coffy show her utilizing her two major strategies of resistance to the criminality in her community: sex and violence. The first photograph depicts her using her sexuality to get the attention of her target, a white man (figure 3.2). She also has the attention of the black man and white woman in the picture. The second photograph brings together both sex and violence as Coffy is wearing a revealing dress while she practices aiming her gun (figure 3.3).

Like in *Coffy*, in one of Grier's most well-known films, *Foxy*
Brown, the main character uses vigilante justice to get revenge. The plot of the film revolves around Foxy's attempts to get revenge for the death of her boyfriend, an undercover cop whose cover was compromised by Foxy's brother. After her lover's death, Foxy goes undercover as a prostitute for Miss Katherine, a ruthless white drug dealer and pimp who is responsible for her boyfriend's death. Like Coffy, Foxy uses her feminine wiles and beauty to facilitate her ultimate act of revenge. The establishing shot that introduces the main character emphasizes the display of her body. In scenes like this, the black female heroine's latent danger is minimized by her erotic appeal. *Foxy Brown*'s opening sequence features Grier dancing in a bikini and a tight leather outfit. There are also numerous gratuitous opportunities for her character to undress and/or otherwise solicit the gaze of other characters. The perception of sexual availability is an important aspect of Grier's performance in *Foxy Brown*, including sexual availability to the men and women within the film and members of the audience. In *Foxy Brown*, Grier's character is given the once-over by Miss Katherine, the head of a prostitution ring. As they discuss Foxy's potential as a member of her operation, shot-reverse-shot is used to show Miss Katherine "checking out" Foxy.[14]

Another important aspect of Grier's performance in the film is the way that the lead character shifts between two opposing images. When playing Sexy Foxy, Grier wears revealing, ultra-feminine clothes (figure 3.4). Foxy is depicted wearing an Afro when she is her most fierce. In contrast, when Foxy wears her straight long wig, she is in undercover mode, hiding the true Foxy as a means to trick her enemies into letting down their guard. The perception that Foxy is harmless is facilitated by fashion choices, including the wig, revealing dress, and high heels that are used to masquerade the stereotypical dangerousness that marks the black woman—big Afro, pants, and a fearless attitude.

52   Narratives within blaxploitation films attempt to ameliorate anxieties provoked by black revolutionary women. It is no accident that these films gained popularity during a time when revolutionary African American women, such as Angela Davis, were being pursued and criminalized by the government and the

FIGURE 3.4
Promotional Poster for Foxy Brown *(1974)*

mainstream media culture. *Foxy Brown* was released in 1974, the same year that Elaine Brown, the first woman to chair the Black Panther Party, took over after Bobby Seale resigned and Huey Newton was exiled to Cuba.[15] The emerging leadership of African American women in black nationalist organizations, as well as the larger feminist movement, made the country ripe to pursue the new and improved, more palpable revolutionary women highlighted in blaxploitation films like *Foxy Brown*. These films reflected and produced anxieties about the consequences of black female aggression. They also contributed to existing narratives about feminists and black revolutionaries that reinforced mass paranoia about the potential dangers facing middle-class America because of radical feminists, black men, and black women taking up arms.

Foxy Brown and *Coffy* reinforce the notion that African American women are a threat, while simultaneously redirecting the focus of their aggression onto othered whites—whites who are drug dealers, prostitutes, lesbians, and those who participate in interracial dating.[16] These deviant white characters play a regular part in blaxploitation films and are almost always the primary targets of the heroine's rage. The placement of these characters in the narrative as well as their ultimate fates constitute a subtle form of scapegoating that suggests to the audience that the system of governance in the United States is not the problem. They suggest that the real threat comes from black criminals and deviant whites who join them in their rampage on the black community. In addition to encouraging racist and sexist scapegoating, stereotypical black and white characters support classist assumptions about inner-city communities.

In addition to occupying the boundary between the status quo and marginalized communities, black female heroines in blaxploitation films often negotiate their needs as women with the needs of men and the larger African American community. Within these films fighting white dominance is defined as complete allegiance to the community, sometimes at the expense

54   of one's individual needs and desires as a woman. In this space, black female characters like Foxy serve as protector of the race through a disavowal or sacrifice of their own needs. The following scene highlights this phenomenon.

Foxy comes to the local black community organization to ask for help with toppling Miss Katherine. As Foxy waits to hear the decision of this all-male council, she is seated in a room. In the room are posters that reference women in the black power movement, specifically a drawing of what appears to be a woman who resembles Kathleen Cleaver or Angela Davis. In addition, there is a nude poster of a black woman who ushers Foxy into this male-dominated space. In this way, the black female body serves as a bridge between androcentric black nationalism and a formulation of nationalism that is more attuned and responsive to the needs of black women.[17]

In the room where the men are gathered is another poster appearing to portray Angela Davis. It is important that this poster is in the background and is overshadowed by the male council. Again, this depiction of black nationalism privileges a male perspective, while diminishing the existence of black revolutionary women who were actively engaged in every aspect of the civil rights struggle. On the other hand, the presence of the picture within the context of this film further solidifies the importance of Davis as an iconic symbol of black revolutionary activism during this time. The mise-en-scène of this scene illustrates another way that the representation of the black revolutionary female in blaxploitation films works to simultaneously contain and reify the image of African American female revolutionaries.

The privileging of the needs of men and the community is presented vividly in *Foxy Brown* through Foxy's revenge. Foxy is being held captive by two white men in a shack in a remote area. She is tied to the bed, bruised, and struggling to get free. There is a scene in which one of the men attacks Foxy and sexually assaults her. She eventually escapes and burns her captors in the shack where she was being held. Although she was drugged, beaten, and raped, her escape and final act of vengeance are framed in terms of her desire to make the criminals pay for the death of her boyfriend. In *Foxy Brown*, rather than constructing the murders of the white men in the film as part of a rape revenge scenario, the narrative minimizes the suffering of the black female character who is raped in favor of a narrative that privileges justice for the black male character.[18] This scene minimizes the pain of bruised, enslaved, and raped women, with little recognition of the harm caused to these women. Instead, there is an emphasis on the role of African American women as mediators between African American men and the larger white society. They also reinforce a narrative that encourages women's bodily sacrifice for a movement that does not necessarily highlight their needs or concerns.

In addition to mediating between blacks and whites, black female revolutionaries are contained through their juxtaposition with white female characters in the films.[19] Many of the blaxploitation films featuring a female heroine have a white female villain or nemesis. These depictions serve to diminish any potential political affinity that may exist between black women and white women, while simultaneously realigning African American women with a struggle focused exclusively on race consciousness.[20] In *Foxy Brown*, the protagonist's white female nemesis controls a brothel that provides the ammunition used to convince prominent officials to "go easy" on drug offenders. It is significant that these films were released during the height of the second wave of the feminist movement, which was overwhelmingly associated with white women, despite the fact that women of color were engaged in feminist activism. Therefore, it is not surprising that these films represented white women as pathological and criminal. The construction of a binary relationship between the image of the black female heroine and the white female villain is part of a larger historical perception of feminism as incompatible with antiracist goals. The blaxploitation film's emphasis on racial tensions and the fight to overcome

56   racism and poverty reinforces a strict separation of the goals of
black liberation and feminism.[21]

Closely related to the conflict between white and black
women in these films are the ways that black women are used
to contain the threat of lesbianism. Black female characters in
many blaxploitation films display open hostility to lesbians,
usually depicted as white. In particular, the perceived corrupt-
ing influence of lesbians on black women is a concern that is
reflected in the plots of these films.[22] The "red herring of lesbian
baiting" is used to obscure the simultaneity of racial and sexual
oppression and convince African American women that aligning
themselves with feminism is unnecessary and dangerous.[23]

Another example of the denial of black lesbian existence
and the demonization of white lesbians occurs in the famous bar
scene in *Foxy Brown*. In this scene, a fight ensues after Foxy's black
female friend is approached by a white lesbian in the bar. This is
important because the scene highlights the overwhelming presence of white lesbians as a threat to the two heterosexual black
women. Foxy's friend is particularly vulnerable because she is
clearly intoxicated, and Foxy is the only one who can rescue her
from becoming prey to the butch lesbian who pursues her. The
absence of black lesbians in the bar denies black lesbianism as
well as the existence of a multicultural lesbian community.

In rare cases when black lesbians are depicted in blaxploitation films, they are masculinized. In a scene in *Coffy*, the title
character seeks out the white female prostitute, whose former
pimp is her next target. Before letting Coffy in, she comments
that her "old man" just left and will be back soon. Ultimately,
a confrontation ensues and Coffy threatens to cut her with a
broken bottle if she does not tell her where he keeps his secret
supply of drugs. The prostitute's "old man" and pimp—a black
woman—enters and accuses her lover of cheating. She then proceeds to chase Coffy from the scene.[24]

Narratives about white female criminality and lesbianism in
blaxploitation films served several functions. They reinforced

the notion that African Americans, especially women, could not and should not trust white women. This idea diverted attention from the larger white patriarchal system, which was primarily responsible for the subjugation of black people. These narratives served as warnings about the dangers of allowing women to have unbridled access to and power in the public sphere, while simultaneously warning about the temptations of same-sex attraction in women-only spaces. Finally, because black women rarely played lesbian characters in blaxploitation films, the existence of black lesbians was denied.

In addition to the various ways that blaxploitation films marginalized lesbians and constructed the feminist movement as only about white women, actresses who starred in these films had to assure the black community that they were not feminists. The August 9, 1973, issue of *Jet* features Grier on the cover. She wears a red blouse that is unbuttoned and tied just above her waistline. She stands facing the camera with her hands on her hips and her mouth opened slightly, embodying her most famous filmic characters, Coffy and Foxy Brown. Grier is asked several questions that illustrate the anxiety about feminism. For example, the interviewer asks "What attracts you about a man?"[25] This question assumes and affirms the public assumption that Grier is heterosexual. These questions seek to contain and claim Grier for a black heterosexual demographic. More specifically, the questions focus on her appeal to the black male audience, assuring the masses of African American men that Grier is heterosexual. When Grier responds that "what comes out of [a man's] head" is what attracts her, the interviewer is concerned and asks if Grier dates only "intellectuals." Grier reassures the interviewer and the audience that she is not exclusively interested in intellectuals and would date "teachers, postmen, truck drivers or cab drivers."[26] Not only does her response assure black men that she is straight, it also assures the readers that she does not allow class concerns to influence her decisions about which men to date.

Another important part of this interview focuses on Grier's relationship to feminism. The interviewer wants to confirm that Grier's strength and single status have nothing to do with feminist consciousness. After discussing why she believes that marriage is not necessarily important, Grier is confronted with, "But you're not into women's lib. . . ."[27] She responds,

> No, but I can dig where they're coming from. It's just that Black women were doing their thing way back in history. The race wouldn't have survived otherwise.[28]

Grier continues with a discussion of Nancy Friday's *My Secret Garden: Women's Sexual Fantasies*, a book based on interviews with women about their sexual fantasies.[29] Grier uses her discussion of this book to illuminate why she thinks black women are stronger than white women and by extension why black women do not need the women's liberation movement. Grier explains her thoughts about the women's movement:

> [Nancy Friday] interviewed quite a few sisters. They were much freer than the white women she interviewed. Black women were thinking and talking about that long before the white women were about to . . . because they were stronger in many ways. But Black women never talked about it around men or older women because of the religious thing.[30]

What is striking about this conversation is the way that Grier's response simultaneously affirms women's liberation while distancing herself and other African American women from mainstream feminism, which was perceived as for white women. She also reinforces the myth that black women are inherently stronger and freer that white women, which in turn emphasizes the notion that black women do not need feminism.[31] Her responses reveal how Grier's early career required her to manage the images of the sexy, angry, and vengeful black women with which she was associated.[32]

Like the situations faced by Michelle Obama and Angela Davis, Grier was faced with an interviewer who had an agenda. She negotiated this by affirming the historical activism of black

women whom she believed were responsible for the survival of
the race. This satisfied her questioner and readers who won-
dered about her allegiance to the African American community.
Her answer shifted the attention away from an interrogation
about her individual views to a focus on the health and survival
of black people as a whole. In this way she distanced herself from
the stereotype of the angry feminist, while maintaining her support of black women's activism.

Another way to understand the multiple functions and
meaning of blaxploitation films featuring Grier is through attention to spectatorship.[33] Attention to the ways that black men and
women, as well as other interpretive communities,[34] respond to
Pam Grier is important to understanding how these films could
empower African American women.[35] On the one hand there
were those who saw the representations as negative, while some
admitted that these films were powerfully alluring and pleasurable.[36] The negotiation of the negative with the positive was an
important part of the way that African American women related
to blaxploitation films.[37]

The pleasurable negotiation of the negative stereotypes
and the empowering aspects of these images are facilitated in
various ways. Blaxploitation films provide an example of black
women displaying a level of agency unfettered by the control
of others. Despite using sex and violence to achieve their goals,
these female protagonists are skilled strategists who identify
their targets, devise a systematic plan of attack, and imple-
ment that plan. Finally, these characters serve as vehicles for
black women to escape into a world where they can experience the liberation of embracing that which is wild, untamed,
and dangerous within them. By using an oppositional gaze and
refocusing their attention on the empowering aspects of these
representations, African American women redefined these
images for their own purposes.[38]

Such an alternative reading and production of meaning is
apparent in Etang Inyang's filmic homage to Pam Grier, *Badass*

Supermama (1996). A close reading of this film shows one way that Grier's films were appropriated and utilized by a black lesbian spectator,[39] and also refutes the assertion made by black male film scholars that black women could find little to identify with in Grier's films.[40]

Inyang makes her identification with Grier clear when she asserts in the opening of *Badass Supermama* that she, like many young girls, was "searching for a mirror, a true reflection of [herself]." While she readily admits that she "had a crush" on Foxy, she also admits that Pam Grier's performance as Foxy Brown "scared the shit out of [her]." The mixture of desire and fear is an important aspect of the appeal of these films for Inyang. The tension between wanting to be Grier and wanting to possess Grier is another important feature of *Badass Supermama*.[41] By explicitly using her voice within the film to read *Foxy Brown* against the grain, Inyang asserts her authority to claim Foxy and Grier as her own, both as a role model and a lover. In addition to using her voice to interrogate Grier and the film, Inyang inserts her own body into Grier's films, thus claiming a space for black lesbians.

In another scene, Inyang positions herself as a member of the audience in a theatre gazing at Grier in *Foxy Brown*. Through this device, she reminds the viewer of the central role that black women play as spectators of Hollywood cinema. While engaging with disturbing images of rape, torture, and women battling women, Inyang tells us that she needs to "reinvent what [she] sees" in order to embrace Foxy and Grier as her own. Through her authorial role as director and her position as a fan and spectator, Inyang carves out a space where African American women can construct their own versions of black womanhood. Her insertion of herself into the famous bar scene in *Foxy Brown* is a meditation on where a black lesbian fits in when all the white women in the bar are lesbian and all the straight women are black. She cowers in the corner as the women fight each other, black against white, gay against straight. However, through the insertion of her dialogue she pleads with the forces that define lesbian identity and

African American identity as mutually exclusive. This is particularly crucial because Inyang's primary object of desire, Grier, is constructed as violently against lesbians in this visual text. Foxy is the character who rushes in to save her friend from the advances of a butch white lesbian. She is also the heroine in the story. She is the figure in the text whom Inyang wants to identify with. As a spectator, she must negotiate the simultaneous acknowledgment and denial of her identity.

Identification is also apparent in Inyang's decision to do a parody of *Foxy Brown*, by donning an Afro wig in her film. It is significant that she chooses this representation of Grier's image to emulate instead of wearing a straight, long wig, another incarnation of the Foxy Brown character. Perhaps by embodying the more militant African American persona of Foxy, Inyang identifies with the strength, power, independence, and revolutionary potential of the character. Her film shows the ways that desire is negotiated simultaneously with a critical evaluation of the medium of blaxploitation and the construction of characters played by Grier.

To further explore the differences between the ways that male spectators and female spectators, particularly lesbian spectators, consume Pam Grier's image, a comparison of the use of her image by Quentin Tarantino and that by Etang Inyang is instructive. Both directors appropriate Grier's star image and persona into their work. Like directors of her earlier films, Tarantino uses techniques from blaxploitation film in his Grier tribute film, *Jackie Brown*.

Tarantino's desire as a "superfan" and "recycler" of icons of mass memory drives his use and depiction of Pam Grier's performance and star image in *Jackie Brown*.[42] Pam Grier plays Jackie Brown, an airline flight attendant who is stuck between a rock and a hard place. She has been caught by federal agents smuggling money from Mexico for Ordell (played by Samuel Jackson), a dealer of illegal guns. She devises a plan to avoid prison and steal Ordell's money. Her bail bondsman, Max Cherry, played by

62 Robert Forster, assists her. Tarantino sees himself as part of a process of reigniting the career of Pam Grier, and other actors who were popular during the blaxploitation era. His project is fueled by his enjoyment of Grier and the blaxploitation genre. In an interview about the film, he shares his admiration of Grier:

> I've just been a big fan for a long time. She is truly a great icon, and she holds a very special place in cinema history. When the blaxploitation phenomenon was going on in the '70s, you had Jim Brown, probably their single biggest star, and they would always say about Brown that he's sort of the black Clint Eastwood. Fred Williamson had the mantle of the black Burt Reynolds; Jim Kelly was the black Bruce Lee. But Pam Grier wasn't a black version of anybody, because there had never been a heroine who specialized in doing action movies, a full-on woman who didn't try to act like a man. Not until women in Hong Kong movies started doing kung fu did that kind of role come up again.[43]

Tarantino's comment points to the iconic status of Pam Grier and illustrates his desire for her. While he does not appear in *Jackie Brown*, he is nonetheless an important presence in the film. For example, his voice is used as the computerized voice on the answering machine located in Jackie's bedroom. More importantly, Tarantino uses the camera and the plot of *Jackie Brown* to capture and claim Grier for himself and other white men.

In the opening sequence of *Jackie Brown*, Tarantino emulates early Grier films, like *Foxy Brown*, that encourage the audience to revel in the beauty and power that she embodies. This scene asks the reader to invest the lead character with the same beauty, grace, power, and strength that is associated with Grier. The camera follows her as she walks confidently through the airport. According to Tarantino, "the first half of the opening credit establishes Pam Grier's power and strength." He says,

> The second half establishes the reality of Jackie Brown's character. . . . After the bad-ass opening credit sequence, two minutes later she's serving peanuts. It starts off as this mythical superhero figure, and then by the end of the credit sequence we've brought it back down to earth.[44]

In many ways, Tarantino tries to represent a "real" African American woman facing a horrible dilemma. However, his nostalgic use of elements from the blaxploitation genre and his clear admiration of Grier, leave the fantasy of Foxy Brown somewhat intact. This connection between Tarantino's film and the genre is illustrated in the promotional poster used to market the film (figure 3.5). In this poster, we see a reworking of the visual

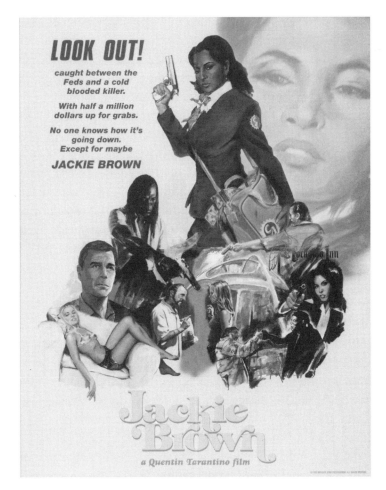

FIGURE 3.5
Promotional Poster for Jackie Brown

64 markers that were used in the posters for *Coffy* and *Foxy Brown*. Jackie looms over the other characters, like the poster for *Coffy*, but she is fully clothed. The depictions of Ordell (a black man) and Max (a white man) are approximately the same size. The bottom-left corner features the white female character played by Bridget Fonda, scantily clad and lounging seductively in a chair. The poster contains three depictions of Jackie. In addition to the central figure, there is close-up of her face directly behind her, and in the bottom-right corner there is a drawing of Jackie shooting her gun. The number of depictions of Jackie in the poster suggests a complexity that was lacking in Grier's earlier films.

However, there are major differences between Foxy Brown and Tarantino's lead character. Jackie works in conjunction with white men. This is a huge departure from *Foxy Brown*. While Grier uses her feminine wiles to trick white men and ultimately to triumph in her blaxploitation films, as Jackie she works with Max Cherry, a white man, to escape the clutches of the federal agents and Ordell, a black man. In this way, Tarantino uses the narrative structure of his film to recuperate the radical black female superheroine for white men. There are numerous scenes where Max watches Jackie from a distance. When Max comes to post Jackie's bond, the camera moves in slowly as he watches her approaching him. The scene is accompanied by a track of the romantic soul classic "Natural High." This song is used throughout the film to signify Max's growing attraction to Jackie. In the original screenplay, the film was to end with a kiss between Pam Grier and Robert Forster.[45] Presumably, this scene would imply that their relationship continues. However, at the end of the film, Tarantino uses a shot of Jackie kissing Max and driving off into the sunset. This change suggests that given the historical reception of Pam Grier's strong and independent roles, such an ending would be more palatable to spectators who remember her early performances. It also reinforces the stereotypical image of the angry, vengeful, black woman that revolutionary African American women in the public have had to confront.

While Tarantino reinforces many of the stereotypical images present in classic blaxploitation film, Etang Inyang subverts the stereotype of the angry black woman as part of a process of claiming a space for black lesbians in narratives about strong black women. The consumption and celebration of these texts illustrate not only the power of the sexualized and objectified image of the angry, black, revolutionary woman in film to avert anxieties about African American women but also the ways that African American female spectators and revolutionary directors, like Etang Inyang, impose their own interpretations, images, and narratives on blaxploitation film as a way to subvert the power of these negative filmic depictions. Through claiming the archetype of the angry black woman and using it to their advantage, black female spectators, directors, and actresses harness the power of the image to achieve their own goals as creative artists and participants in American popular culture.

4

REVOLUTIONARY BLACK WOMEN
IN LITERATURE
The Narratives of Alice Walker and
Audre Lorde

In June 1982, *Ebony* featured an article by Bebe Moore Campbell that asked the question, what happened to the Afro?[1] Campbell chronicles the shift from popular culture saturated with images of black men and women wearing this natural hairstyle to one where large numbers of African American women were returning to the practice of straightening their hair.[2] In addition to the decline of natural hairstyles, there was also a drop in the number of mass-produced images of black revolutionary women like those that circulated in the popular media of the seventies. Despite becoming relatively obscure in mainstream popular culture, images of strong, revolutionary black women remained a central and important part of the work of African American activists, artists, and scholars during the eighties. Writers such as Audre Lorde and Alice Walker contributed significantly to depictions of black revolutionary women by constructing images of African American women who intervened in debates about black womanhood and provided inspiration for the work produced by young African American female artists in the 1990s.[3] The images constructed by Lorde and Walker in their written texts, as well as their influence as iconic figures in black feminist thought, were an important outcome of the explosion

68 of interest in the writing of African American women during this time. An analysis of several images and scenes in Walker's *The Color Purple* along with its filmic adaptation and Lorde's *Zami: A New Spelling of My Name* illustrates how literary representations of black revolutionary womanhood provided an important bridge between visual representations in the seventies and the work of young African American women in the nineties. Lorde's and Walker's works spoke to these and other black women and provided a foundation that allowed for new depictions of black revolutionary female activism.[4]

The construction of both Audre Lorde and Alice Walker as public figures in feminist and antiracist activism is an essential part of understanding the impact of their written work. There was controversy surrounding Walker's novel *The Color Purple*, which was later adapted into a film.[5] Most recently, Walker's novel was made into a Broadway play produced by Oprah Winfrey and Quincy Jones. Some critics of Walker's novel portrayed her as a radical and angry woman who was participating in the public airing of the dirty laundry,[6] of intraracial rape, incest, and domestic violence in the African American community.[7] Within the feminist community, she was heralded as the quintessential black feminist, partially due to her unabashed willingness to claim feminism, redefined as womanism,[8] in the face of mounting criticism from African American critics, many male, who saw her work as incompatible with the black liberation struggle. Similarly, Audre Lorde used her work to challenge sexism and heterosexism in the black community and confronted racism within the ranks of feminist organizations.[9] She also pushed African American women to examine how homophobia was used to separate them from each other.[10] Audre Lorde's construction of herself as a "warrior poet" was a part of her active resistance to the marginalization of black feminist lesbians. Lorde critiqued the way that African American gays and lesbians were rendered invisible in the civil rights movement, inspiring many to break the silences that rendered them invisible in these organizations.[11] Her biomythography, *Zami: A New Spelling of My Name*, is a concrete example of the way that she used the image of the Amazon to construct a legacy of black womanhood that has always included black lesbians. Characters in texts by Alice Walker and Audre Lorde not only work on a written level but also allow for a visual imagination of revolution that has remained salient in the work of African American female artists today.[12]

Unlike the filmic representations of African American women in blaxploitation films from the seventies that denied the vulnerability of black women, the writing of African American women in the eighties showcased a nuanced and complex portrait of black female strength tempered by vulnerability. Black female characters in blaxploitation films, such as *Foxy Brown*, could be beaten, drugged, and raped and emerge seemingly with no scars ready to continue their battles. In contrast, Walker and Lorde produced characters whose pain in the face of abuse is salient. In others words, the strength of these characters coexists with vulnerability in a world that often views black women as invulnerable to the harsh realities of oppression. Walker clearly rejects the myth of the black superwoman,[13] and does not sugarcoat the real consequences of revolutionary struggle in the lives of black women.[14] Lorde creates portraits of black women who encounter social injustices and who stand in the gap between the young Lorde and the chaos of the world. She emphasizes that it is the "images of women, kind and cruel" that led her home and made it possible for her to survive.[15] Both Walker and Lorde celebrate strong black women without relying on the stereotype of the angry black woman, while simultaneously constructing complex female characters who embody strength and ferocity in the face of injustice. These characters clearly hurt and at the same time resist their subordination and destruction.

Alice Walker's novel *The Color Purple* has two important characters that represent revolutionary women in her text, Shug Avery and Sofia. In this way, the book functions as a revolutionary text.[16] The main character, Celie, learns from them by observing, which moves her from oppression to resistance. Celie's development into a strong woman who can resist the abuse of her husband is partially facilitated through her interactions with Shug Avery, her husband's mistress, and Sofia, her daughter-in-law. Walker makes it clear that Celie is not a fighter,[17] and contrasts her with these two characters who refuse to conform to conventional standards of womanhood. Walker uses the mythological image of the Amazon to construct the character of Sofia.[18] We first encounter Sofia when Harpo, Celie's stepson, brings Sofia home so that his father, Mister, can "have a look at her,"[19] a gesture toward the visual scrutiny of black women as potential wives and mothers. Sofia and Harpo are in love, but her pregnancy is the catalyst that allows the marriage to proceed. She and Harpo march hand in hand up the road to the house, with Sofia in front "like going to war,"[20] the first time in the text that Walker constructs Sofia as a fighter. This is followed by a description of Sofia's physical appearance. Celie explains,

> Harpo so black he think [Sofia] bright, but she ain't that bright. Clear medium brown skin, gleam on it like on good furniture. Hair notty but a lot of it, tied up on her head in a mass of plaits. She not quite as tall as Harpo but much bigger, and strong and ruddy looking, like her mama brought her up on pork.[21]

Walker's description of Sofia's dark skin color and notty hair is linked to her lack of submissiveness to male authority. As the novel develops, we learn that Sofia will not submit to Harpo's attempts to control her. Harpo is distraught because he believes that his wife should submit to his authority, and Celie advises Harpo to beat Sofia.[22] Harpo's attempt to control Sofia through violence results in physical altercations, which Walker describes as like watching two men in a fight.[23] Again we see the association of Sofia with rejection of traditional femininity and gender roles and violent resistance to male aggression. Later in the text, Sofia confronts Celie about her advice to Harpo. This confrontation emphasizes Sofia's construction as an iconic revolutionary Amazonian woman. Sofia says,

> All my life I had to fight. I had to fight my daddy. I had to fight my brothers. I had to fight my cousins and my uncle. A girl child ain't safe in a family of men. . . . I loves Harpo, she say. God knows I do. But I'll kill him dead before I let him beat me. Now if you want a dead son-in-law you just keep on advising him like you doing. . . . I used to hunt game with a bow and arrow, she say.[24]

When Sofia decides to leave Harpo, her sisters come to retrieve her and her belongings. Celie writes, "Sofia right about her sisters. They all big strong healthy girls, look like amazons."[25]

The image of Sofia using a bow and arrow, her physical resistance to spousal abuse, as well as the description of her sisters solidify Walker's construction of Sofia as an Amazonian warrior. Walker could have used a gun but instead chose to associate Sofia's defiance with a warrior sensibility that is rooted in a female community.

In addition to Sofia, Walker's description of Shug Avery, Mister's mistress and famous blues singer,[26] and Celie's fascination with her and their love affair are essential parts of the novel. Walker's treatment of this romantic triangle challenges the privileging of black male desire and engages an explicit discourse about same-sex attraction and intimacy that becomes a central theme in the novel. Celie is fascinated with Shug, a fascination that is not new. In fact, Walker shows us the seeds of Celie's fascination with Shug early in the text when Celie overhears her father and Mister discussing the availability of her younger sister, Nettie, for marriage. In the process, Shug Avery is mentioned. When Celie asks her mom about Shug, she shows Celie a photograph that Celie clings to and sleeps with at night.[27] Walker's introduction of Shug through the visual is extremely important because it highlights the strong bridge between the written and the visual that this novel allows. In addition, later in the text Celie dresses like Shug to prevent her father from raping her sister, Nettie.[28] She sacrifices herself by imitating the visual representation of Shug.[29] Both these scenes emphasize seeing and performance as essential aspects of Celie's attraction and fascination with Shug. They also reinforce the important function of the visual and the later emergence of Celie's revolutionary consciousness within the text.

When Shug comes to town, Celie is as excited as her husband about seeing Shug. Celie describes the pink flyer announcing the return of Shug as "burning a hole" in her pocket.[30] Celie's burning pocket represents Celie's sexual desire for Shug that later develops into an affair between the two characters. Later in the book, Shug comes to stay with Celie and Mister because she is ill. Celie is fascinated by her and eager to take care of her needs and thinks that it is ridiculous that Mister is afraid to bathe a woman with whom he has fathered three children.[31] Celie eagerly volunteers to nurse her husband's mistress back to health. While she is bathing her, Celie studies Shug's "long black body" and thinks that she has turned into a man. Shug tells her to take a good look and poses for Celie.[32] Again Celie's desire for Shug is clear. As she washes Shug, her hands tremble and she feels like she has been praying.[33] When she prepares and serves Shug breakfast, she thinks, "If I don't watch out I'll have hold of her hand, tasting her fingers in my mouth."[34] Shug drinks coffee, smokes, and looks at white women in a magazine as Celie bathes her.[35] Again, Walker uses the visual to further explore Celie's attraction to Shug and as a way of critiquing white standards of beauty. She does this by juxtaposing Shug's reading of white women's magazines and Celie's thoughts about Shug's beauty. Celie observes,

> She is busy looking at a magazine. White women in it laughing, holding they beads out on one finger, dancing on top of motorcars. Jumping into fountains. She flips the pages. Look dissatisfied. Remind me of a child trying to git something out of a toy it can't work yet.[36]

This scene highlights the importance of magazines in the construction of feminine beauty. It also suggests the inability of African American women to gain much from focusing on imitating mainstream Eurocentric images of femininity. This is further

REVOLUTIONARY BLACK WOMEN IN LITERATURE

emphasized in the following scene when Celie washes and combs Shug's hair. Celie says that Shug "got the nottiest, shortest, kinkiest hair [she] ever saw, and [she] loves every strand of it. The hair that come out in [her] comb [she] kept."[37] Through Walker's description of Celie combing Shug's kinky hair, she recognizes the function of hair in the development of intimacy among black women. Her description also celebrates the beauty of natural hair. Celie's careful attention to grooming Shug would eventually "scratch a song out of her head" that she would later dedicate to Celie.[38]

After recuperating and again able to perform, Shug sings at Harpo's juke joint. Shug chooses a song by Bessie Smith, another famous blues singer whom she claims to know.[39] This reference to Bessie Smith is important because she as well as other blues singers, like Gertrude "Ma" Rainey, were rumored to have been sexually involved with women. Celie describes how jealous and hurt she feels when Shug looks at Mister while she sings.[40] She wants to have Shug look at her in the same way. Shortly thereafter, Shug acknowledges Celie and sings the song that she scratched out of Shug's head.[41] Again, looking and visual performance are emphasized in the novel.

Shug teaches Celie to love herself through the visual. Shug and Celie discuss sex and the fact that Celie does not enjoy sex. Celie knows nothing about the sexual aspects of her body, and Shug cannot believe that Celie is afraid to look at herself.[42] Shug encourages Celie to look at her vagina using a mirror and explains the pleasure that can come from stimulating her clitoris.[43] Shug says, "It a lot prettier than you thought, ain't it?"[44] Later that night, Celie masturbates as she listens to Shug and Albert having sex.[45] Later in the text, Celie and Shug become lovers.[46] Walker makes their love relationship and building of a life together a central aspect of her book. When the novel was made into a film, with the exception of an on-screen kiss, this complex love relationship was nonexistent.

Despite the controversial topics and raw portrayals of the experiences of African American women in Walker's novel, there

74   was still interest in making *The Color Purple* into a film. The adaptation of Alice Walker's novel into a film and a Broadway play suggests the extent to which black women's literature evokes and compels visualization.[47] The inclination of producers such as Oprah Winfrey to represent visually these fictional works suggests that the invisibility of black women that texts such as *The Color Purple* tried to overcome actually worked not simply on a written level but also in the realm of the visual. These texts yell "See me!" and filmic adaptation provided that opportunity. Film also provided a critical way to expose the masses of people who would not otherwise read texts like *The Color Purple* to the important work of African American women writers.

In the filmic adaptation of *The Color Purple* (1985), Walker, Steven Spielberg, and Quincy Jones visually bring to life the characters in her book. Despite not writing the screenplay, Walker played a central role in the process of adapting her novel into a film.[48] The film features scenes of beauty, such as young Celie (played by Whoopi Goldberg) and her sister playing patty-cake in a field, and scenes of brutality and horror, particularly when Celie is sexually and physical abused. There are also moments in the film that celebrate the ability of African American women to resist oppression. For example, consider the scene where Celie shaves Mister. She had just been slapped by Mister (played by Danny Glover) while she was in the process of secretly reading letters from her sister that Mister refused to give her. The tension in the film is heightened by the sounds of African drumming and singing and is juxtaposed with an initiation ritual in Africa that involves the cutting of marks on the faces of male and female initiates. This scene becomes particularly revolutionary in the way that the audience is encouraged to watch Celie's inner warrior woman emerge as she prepares the knife to shave mister. The camera focuses on the visible anger on Celie's face and the methodical way that she sharpens the knife. She has been warned several times throughout the film not to accidentally cut Mister. However, this is the first time in the film we see Celie transformed from a scared child into a potentially dangerous woman. Because of her discovery of his most harmful treachery, keeping her from her sister, and her realization that she has the power to free herself from Mister, she is able to perceive the razor not as grooming tool but instead as a revolutionary tool to escape her oppressor. The negotiation between the desire to kill and humanistic values comes to a head as we see Shug (played by Margaret Avery) running through the fields to stop Celie. Shug, Mister and Celie's lover, intuitively senses Celie's rage and homicidal intent. As tension builds in the scene and Celie raises her hand to "shave" Mister, Shug grabs her hand at this critical moment and prevents the slaughter. This will not be the last time that Celie confronts mister with a knife.

At one of several dinner scenes in the film, Shug announces that she, her husband, and Celie are leaving. Mister asserts his male authority as husband and forbids Celie to leave. He and his father laugh and joke about the foolishness of Celie thinking that she could leave her husband. This jovial interaction is abruptly interrupted by Celie, who stabs her knife into the table and threatens her abusive husband by holding the knife to his neck.[49] The knife is a symbol of male power and the subordination of women throughout the novel. Celie is no longer using a blade to shave her husband or to chop food for feeding his family. Instead, she uses the knife as a warrior to draw a very clear boundary between herself and the authority of her husband. The camera tightens in on the fear in Mister's eyes as Celie asserts herself. This awakening of the warrior in Celie facilitates a "revolution" within the familial unit, as Sofia regains her voice and the fiery spirit—illustrated by her laughter—that the racist justice system has beaten out of her. Squeak (Harpo's mistress) affirms her right to be called by her real name, Mary Alice, and her determination to leave with Shug and Celie to pursue a singing career. In the filmic adaptation, the men are stunned into silence and the women's voices emerge, a turning point for Celie and the other women in the film. They have found their voices and strength while seated at the dining room table. This brings to mind the kitchen table, a site of dialogue and consciousness raising for black women that has been discussed by African American women scholars and celebrated in the creation of companies such as the Kitchen Table: Women of Color Press.[50] The scene emphasizes how the challenging of oppression by even one woman can have a ripple effect, causing other women to reevaluate their situations and rebel against patriarchy.

An earlier scene in the film highlights the power of women and the important role of consciousness raising in their ability to resist oppression. Celie plays "dress-up" and tries on one of Shug's dresses; the red beaded dress associated with being a loose woman who sings worldly music becomes an important symbol of revolution. Because Shug is an independent rebel who refuses to conform to the standards around her, Celie donning her dress is an important visual moment in the film. Through wearing Shug's dress and being forced to reclaim her smile in the mirror, Celie is transformed and is able to see her own beauty and desirability as a woman. Using the mirror as an important device in this scene, the director allows us to experience the genesis of a process of transformation of Celie into a revolutionary figure in the text. Celie becomes Shug for a moment, or at least she sees the reflection of her potential as a revolutionary reflected in the mirror. That this scene is followed by a tender kiss between the two women is important because it symbolizes a women's-only space where intimacy between women is a revolutionary catalyst. The strong negative reaction of some audiences and critics to this very small expression of same-sex love and tenderness shows the revolutionary nature of the scene. It highlights the "uses of the erotic as power"[51] and emphasizes the important role that female intimacy plays in Celie's ability to see herself as a strong, independent woman who has control of her destiny.

In the film the intensity and serious nature of Shug and Celie's relationship were downplayed. However, the kissing scene allows the audience to see the revolutionary potential of female intimacy. The fact that one of the most revolutionary women in the novel and film is a dark blues singer is important given the historical legacy of the blues singer.[52] The association of blues singers with willful and independent female sexuality that challenged interpersonal emotional and physical violence within male/female relationships, as well as the celebration of same-sex love, is a prominent feature of Shug's construction in Walker's novel.

One drawback to the adaptation of texts such as *The Color Purple* is that it takes the vision of one or a few and links it to a text in ways that do not necessarily accurately depict the author's vision. However, the visual adaptation of a text allows these cultural productions to function intertextually. The film and the novel are part of an ongoing play between the visual and the written. Consequently, we see that images of the revolutionary black woman did not disappear; they simply began to proliferate in the literature of African American women. The importance and resonance of the material among black women,[53] as well as the mainstream attention that some of these texts received, allowed them to pass on remnants of revolutionary iconography and rhetoric that would inform the cultural work of young African American women in the nineties.

Walker's critically acclaimed novel and the filmic adaptation had a profound impact on the written and visual legacy of the black revolutionary woman in popular culture. The strong black women in the novel and the film, particularly Sofia and Shug, represent an important part of who Walker is and what she stands for in terms of radical, revolutionary black feminism. In an online transcript featuring an on-stage interview with Amy Goodman during the thirtieth anniversary celebration of Media Alliance in 2006, Amy Goodman asked Walker, "You write in *The Same River Twice: Honoring the Difficult*, 'What I have kept, which the film avoided entirely, is Shug's completely unapologetic self-acceptance as outlaw, renegade, rebel and pagan.' Do you see yourself that way?" Walker responded,

Oh, absolutely. Yes. Why wouldn't I be? I know I'm very soft-spoken, but I have endeavored to live my life by my terms and that means that I am a renegade, an outlaw, a pagan. . . . A rebel, oh yes. Oh yes, and there is no reason not to rebel. I learned that really early. There is no reason whatsoever.[54]

Walker's willingness to explicitly claim the status of rebel suggests that she was not concerned with the ways that an explicit affirmation of her revolutionary nature might be deployed in the service of critics who sought to construct her as angry and bitter. Her use of the descriptors "soft-spoken" and "rebel" to describe herself provided an image of black revolutionary womanhood that did not rely on the stereotypical pairing of radical activism with illegitimate and irrational anger. As she proceeds to discuss the ways that the harsh criticism she received for the book and the film hurt her, she claims her right to be both a strong black woman and someone who hurts. This disrupts the stereotypical image of angry black political activists that was used against Obama and Davis and sexy, homicidal black female heroines in Grier's films. Unlike Michelle Obama's strategy of suppressing any emotional response to attacks against herself and her husband, Walker is very open about her hurt feelings and the time that it took for her to no longer be bothered by the attacks of her critics.[55]

Walker's characterization of herself as "soft-spoken" is reinforced in visual images that depict a serene public image. On the cover of one of her most influential books of essays, *In Search of Our Mothers' Gardens: Womanist Prose*, Walker wears the classic Afro, which was starting to wane in popularity during the eighties, and rests her face against her finger, suggesting that she is in deep thought (figure 4.1). This pose represents her role as a scholar and a thinker but does not seem to capture the radical, pagan rebel with which Walker identifies. Walker smiles warmly into the camera, not depicting the angry attitude associated with revolutionary black women from the seventies. Photographs that depict Walker wearing a crown of flowers over her long dreadlocks capture a less threatening aspect of Walker's persona that seems to obscure her radical threat to the status quo. However, pictures of Walker in nature and wearing flowers (figure 4.2) may indeed reflect Walker's humanist values and her genuine peaceful nature. The dual image of Walker as the radical revolutionary rebel and the humanist adds a more complex narrative about what it means to be a black woman active in the fight for racial justice. It counters the stereotypical image of black female revolutionaries who are angry and dangerous and instead emphasizes that revolutionary activism, peace, and humanistic values are important aspects of the womanist project that Walker represents.

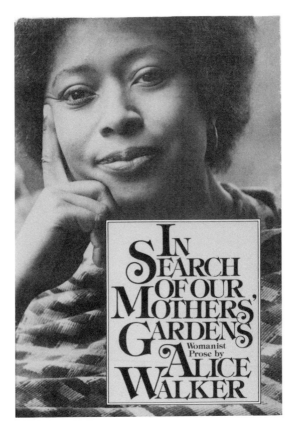

FIGURE 4.1
Cover of Walker's In Search of Our Mothers' Gardens

FIGURE 4.2
Walker with a Crown of Flowers

In a similar way, two pictures of Audre Lorde have come to represent her construction as a revolutionary poet–activist within the feminist community. The first is a well-known picture of Lorde that has been utilized as a poster and printed on T-shirts. This colorful poster features Lorde with raised hands (figure 4.3). Her stance is powerful, and one can imagine several onlookers applauding her presence. Coupled with her African-inspired clothing, this picture clearly illustrates her importance as a symbol of triumph and suggests a certain reverence for her as an important activist for the rights of oppressed people.

The second important image of Lorde is on the cover of her book *Sister Outsider: Essays and Speeches* (figure 4.4). Similar to her depiction on the poster, on this cover she pays homage to African fashion by wearing Kenté cloth draped around her neck. She stares directly at the camera and holds the side of her

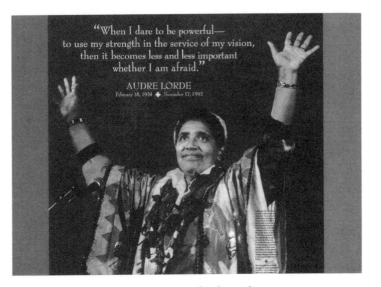

FIGURE 4.3: *Poster of Audre Lorde*
FIGURE 4.4: *Cover of Audre Lorde's* Sister Outsider

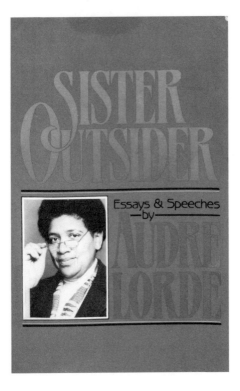

eyeglasses in a gesture suggesting that she is about to impart wisdom to a group of students she is teaching. In no way does this photograph warn of the biting and radical commentary contained within its pages. In the collection of essays that follows, one sees a clear portrait of a scholar and activist committed to confronting various forms of oppression, including racism, sexism, heterosexism, ageism, and classism.

In *Zami: A New Spelling of My Name*, Lorde infuses her identity as a black, lesbian, feminist, disabled poet and cancer survivor into her reflections on and memories of her childhood and growth into womanhood. Lorde's attention to revealing lesbian desire within a variety of contexts allows her to construct a space where black lesbians always existed. Like Walker, Lorde employs the figure of the Amazonian warrior to describe her struggles with the loneliness of being black and gay. She says,

> I remember how being young and Black and gay and lonely felt.... There were no mothers, no sisters, no heroes. We had to do it alone, like our sister Amazons, the riders on the loneliest outposts of the kingdom of Dahomey. We, young and Black and fine and gay, sweated out our first heartbreaks with no school nor office chums to share that confidence over lunch hour.[56]

This connection between the Amazon and black lesbian identity is a consistent theme in *Zami*. Lorde uses a discussion of her mother's difference as a way to understand her own identity. After discussing the ways that her mother was a powerful woman at a time when the "word-combination was almost [inexpressible] in the white American common tongue, except or unless it was accompanied by some aberrant explaining adjective...."[57] Lorde continues,

> As a child, I always knew my mother was different from other women that I knew Black or white. I used to think that it was because she was my mother. But different how? I never was quite sure.... But that is why to this day I believe that there have always been Black dykes around—in the sense of powerful and women-oriented women—who would rather have died than use that name for themselves. And that includes my momma.[58]

Lorde's description of leaving her mother's home at the age
of seventeen is illustrative of the way that she associates her
mother's difference with an inherited warrior sensibility. She
explains,

> I made an adolescent's wild and powerful commitment to battling in
> my own full eye, close to my own strength, which was after all not
> so very different from my mother's. And there I found other women
> who sustained me and from whom I learned other loving. How to
> cook the foods I had never tasted in my mother's house. How to drive
> a stick-shift car. How to loosen up and not be lost. *Their shapes join
> Linda and Gran'Ma Liz and Gran'Aunt Anni in my dreaming, where they
> dance with swords in their hands, stately forceful steps, to mark the time
> they were all warriors.*[59]

Lorde's references to warriors throughout her text are associated with an inheritance she received from her mother and
other female ancestors as well as linked to the women she
encountered throughout her life. These women included friends
and lovers. The image of the Amazon emerges in *Zami* also when
Lorde falls in love with a woman named Eudora, who has lost a
breast due to breast cancer. Lorde describes her love and reverence for Eudora's body:

> Kneeling, I pass my hands over her body, along the now-familiar
> place below her left shoulder, down along her ribs. A part of her. The
> mark of the Amazon. For a woman who seems spare, almost lean,
> in her clothing, her body is ripe and smooth to the touch. Beloved.
> Warm to my coolness, cool to my heat. I bend, moving my lips over
> her flat gentle stomach to the firm rising mound beneath.[60]

During her own battle with breast cancer, Lorde again references the strength of the Amazons when she wonders how fif-
teen-year-old girls could endure the painful removal of one's
breast.[61] Like the mythical Amazons, the missing breast allowed
Lorde and her characters to pull their metaphorical bow against
oppression.

Lorde's clear affirmation of the historical presence of
black lesbians is illustrated by the character of Afrekete. Lorde
explains that Afrekete "taught [her] roots, new definitions of

our women's bodies—definitions for which [she] had only been in training to learn before."[62] Lorde explains that all the women that she had ever loved left a "print" on her life. Her definition of the Zami embraces a complex understanding of lesbian identity and its connection to womanhood. She explains,

> Zami. A Carriacou name for women who work together as friends and lovers. We carry our traditions with us. . . . Recreating in words the women who helped give me substance. Ma-Liz, Delois, Louise Briscoe, Aunt Anni, Linda, and Genevieve; MawuLisa, thunder, sky, sun, the great mother of us all; and Afrekete, her youngest daughter, the mischievous linguist, trickster, best-beloved, whom we must all become. One home was a long way off, a place I had never been to but knew out of my mother's mouth. I only discovered its latitudes when Carriacou was no longer my home. There it is said that the desire to lie with other women is a drive from the mother's blood.[63]

In the final pages of her biomythography, Lorde solidifies black lesbian identity as an important part of her lineage and heritage. In addition, she connects with a women-centered community that includes not only those who take women as lovers but also those who sustain other women spiritually and physically.

Both Audre Lorde and Alice Walker function as revolutionary icons on multiple levels. First, their written work provides the imagery that allows for a reemergence of visual representations of black revolutionary womanhood. Second, both Walker and Lorde provide a clear articulation of a black feminist consciousness during a period of decline in mass involvement in feminist and black nationalist movements. Finally, both authors embody revolutionary iconography. Their public images would become a salient reference point for young female performers trying to negotiate sexism, racism, and homophobia. Both revolutionary writers and activists created a bridge with their work and their personas. They not only represented black womanhood but also constructed a visible image of black womanhood that resonated with African American female artists who were developing their own identities as activists and cultural producers.

Alice Walker and Audre Lorde provided the foundation for the emergence of new creative work by African American women, like Erykah Badu and Me'shell Ndegéocello, who like the black women before them would be faced with stereotypical images. In their literature, Walker and Lorde left a host of new images that countered stereotypical ones: beauty developed not from the pages of white women's magazines that excluded black women; clothing demonstrated character and rebellion rather than seduction; a celebration of black women's intimate relationships and eroticism developed a different source of power; the explicit disavowal of black lesbian experience in the black community was challenged; and black women found their revolutionary voices that invigorated struggles for social justice. The interplay between film and text made these images available to broad and eclectic audiences, countering the negative image of the angry black woman that pervaded American popular culture.

5

REVOLUTIONARY BLACK WOMEN AND MUSIC
The Hip-Hop Feminism of Erykah Badu and Me'shell Ndegéocello

Images of black revolutionary womanhood that emerged in the literature of black feminists Alice Walker and Audre Lorde were an important part of bridging the gap between black feminist politics in the seventies and the work in the early nineties of African American female artists who were part of the emerging genres of rap, hip-hop and neo-soul.[1] While some scholarship on rhythm and blues, rap, and hip-hop music has focused almost exclusively on black male performers, recent scholarship has emphasized the importance of understanding how young female artists use their craft to engage in revolutionary politics while negotiating their spaces within the music industry.[2] Because of the success of *The Color Purple*, Alice Walker was able to influence artists like Erykah Badu who constructed their own versions of black revolutionary womanhood in their music. In fact, Badu used the filmic adaptation of *The Color Purple* as inspiration for the video for her hit song "On & On."[3] Likewise, Audre Lorde's poetry, essays, and biomythography, *Zami: A New Spelling of My Name*, raised awareness about black lesbian identity, politics, and desire and the important role of African American gays and lesbians in black civil rights struggles. Through her music, Me'shell Ndegéocello, an out bisexual

African American woman, continues Lorde's legacy by using her work to combat injustices.

Badu and Ndegéocello use revolutionary iconography as they confront racism, sexism, classism, heterosexism, and a critique of systems of oppression in the United States as well as conflict in the black and feminist movements. The images and lyrics in the music and performances of Badu and Ndegéocello are important parts of understanding how young African American women in the nineties negotiated the intersections of race, gender, nationalism, sexuality, and classism while extending the dialogue about the role of black women in movements for social justice. Through their music and performances Badu and Ndegéocello pay homage not only to the musicians who have inspired their work but also to black revolutionaries who have inspired the political messages in their music. In addition to positioning themselves as part of a legacy of revolutionary black activism, their work can be read as part of a tradition of black feminist theorizing about revolution, justice, and black womanhood. In addition, their cultural productions illustrate the ways that they negotiate the various contradictions within the popular cultural traditions of rap, hip-hop, and neo-soul.[4] This process of theorizing and negotiation is accomplished through strategies of self-definition and naming; embracing a black aesthetic; asserting women's sexual agency; and confronting racism, sexism, classism, and heterosexism as part of their overall commitment to black men and the African American community as a whole.

Self-definition and naming is an important strategy used by Erykah Badu and Me'shell Ndegéocello. Both changed their given names and adopted names that linked them to a tradition of naming that connects African Americans to their African heritage and past.[5] Erykah Badu, formerly Erica Wright, rejected what she calls her "slave name."[6] She negotiated the need to redefine herself with a willingness to respect her mother's wish that she keep her given name. Instead, she changed the spelling as an act of agency and empowerment.[7] She attributes her last name "Badu" to her love of bebop and jazz, which uses improvisation and the practice of scatting.[8] Her willingness to compromise as she claimed her right to redefine herself in opposition to Eurocentric culture shows a tremendous respect for her mother and an affirmation of the othermothers who helped to raise her.[9] Similarly, Me'shell Ndegéocello constructed her professional image partly through her rejection of her Eurocentric name. In a 1996 interview for *Essence*, Ndegéocello (formerly Michelle Johnson) explains that her new last name is derived from a Swahili phrase that means "free like a bird."[10] Like many African American female and male activists before them, both artists renamed themselves as part of a political statement that reflected their commitment to a revolutionary struggle connected to a historical black nationalist tradition. Through renaming, Badu and Ndegéocello signal to their fans and other listeners that they have a revolutionary sensibility that rejects Eurocentrism in favor of an Afrocentric aesthetic.

Early in her career, Badu wore traditional African garb, head wraps, and ethnic jewelry as a way of resisting hegemonic notions of beauty imposed by white supremacist patriarchal society. The wearing of natural hair (in the form of an Afro, braids, or other ethnic hairstyles), like it did in the seventies, links Badu to a tradition of black nationalist politics.[11] Badu's style of dress is a deliberate attempt to express her philosophical approach to life and assert herself as a strong black woman. She explains,

> The way I dress—I love adorning myself with my culture. And it is not a black and white thing for me, but I am very interested in the black community because there are a lot of professional artists and geniuses who dwell in that community who need to be uplifted in some kind of way. . . . I want to be a different example of what a black woman is, what a black person is. I wear my head wrap because a head wrap is a crown, and I am a queen. A head wrap demands a certain amount of respect—it just does, and I am always head wrapped.[12]

This quote highlights Badu's interest in embracing an African aesthetic not only as a celebration of heritage but also as a source of female empowerment. She uses the head wrap to command a certain amount of respect and to signal to others (male and female) that she demands respect not only as a black person but also as a black woman. This message is an important part of her use of revolutionary iconography. On the cover of her first album, *Baduizm* (1997), she is pictured in profile wearing Afrocentric clothing and her signature head wrap (figure 5.1). She holds her head down as she contemplates something that causes her to hold her head. There is something important on her mind. The title, *Baduizm*, brings to mind other terms like *racism* and *sexism*, for which one could argue Badu's philosophy or baduizm is a remedy. In fact, much of her first album is spent raising awareness and consciousness.

Unlike Badu, Me'shell Ndegéocello does not embrace an Afrocentric style of dress. However, she usually shaves her head bald or wears her hair closely cropped. She also uses the lyrics in

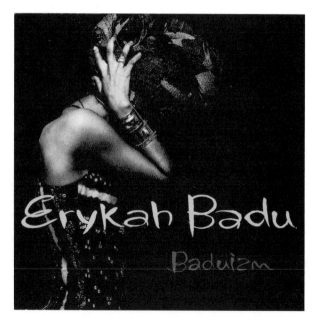

FIGURE 5.1
Cover of Erykah Badu's Baduizm *(1997)*

her songs to celebrate natural hair and a black aesthetic. Her first album, *Plantation Lullabies* (1993), features the love song "Dredlocs," in which she sings about how she loves her male partner's dredlocs.[13] She also critiqued the valorization of Eurocentric standards by black men who date white women in her single "Soul of Ice," which was inspired by the classic book of the same name, written by Black Panther Party leader Eldridge Cleaver. Ndegéocello's nostalgic nod to the black nationalist movement of the seventies is also reflected in a line from her song, "I'm Diggin' You (Like An Old Soul Record)." She says, "Remember back in the day when everybody was black and conscious and down for the struggle?"[14]

Love, relationships, and women's sexuality are important parts of Ndegéocello's and Badu's music. Ndegéocello's approach to men and sexuality is complicated by her very open identification as bisexual. In "Dred Loc," she tells her lover to "rest [his] weary head and let [her] run [her] fingers through [his] dreds." In the chorus, she sings, "let me run my fingers through your dred locs / and rub your body down." This song includes the line "ooh how I love a Black man oh my." The video for the song features shots of Ndegéocello with an African American man with long dredlocs. The intimacy between the two is highlighted by various scenes of the two fully clothed in bed, with Ndegéocello's partner resting his head between her legs as she strokes his head and twirls his dredlocs in her fingers. She and her partner dance, kiss, and hold each other at various points in the video. Like the song, the video is very sensual and features Ndegéocello topless with her arms covering her breasts as she reflects on her love interest. There is also a scene in which Ndegéocello's partner shaves her closely cropped hair. The juxtaposition of a man with long hair and Ndegéocello with a shaved head, along with various points in the video where Ndegéocello plays a more dominant role, forces the viewer to reconsider traditional expressions of femininity and masculinity. However, the overall message of black heterosexual love is still a prominent and important part of Ndegéocello's early work, despite the fact that various elements in her performance hail a gay or lesbian audience.[15]

Erykah Badu expresses sexuality in exclusively heterosexual terms. Her object of desire is always a black man, whom she constructs in her music as a victim of systematic oppression. Badu often sings about the link among inequality, poverty, and criminality. She uses her music to explore the ways that African American women negotiate a desire to support African American men as part of a larger message about the ways that oppression impacts black families and communities. In the song "Other Side of the Game," Badu's protagonist laments the fact that she is pregnant and her partner sells drugs for a living. She sings, "See me and baby got this situation / See brother got this complex occupation / And it ain't that he don't have education / Cause I was there at his graduation."[16] This part of the song attempts to complicate the reasons why some African American men turn to crime as a means of survival. Badu's song poignantly illustrates how difficult it is for an African American woman to negotiate her survival (and her children's survival) with her desire to support the man she loves. In the chorus to "Other Side of the Game," Badu sings,

> What you gon do when they come for you / Work ain't honest but it pays the bills [yes it does] / What you gon do when they come for you / God, I can't stand life without you.[17]

This song emphasizes issues such as poverty, the high rate of imprisonment of African Americans, and a general skepticism about the ability of black people to achieve the American dream. Through her music and her performance, she engages in a process of consciousness raising and uplift that is aimed at the African American community. This rhetoric of "uplifting the race" has been a staple part of how black female activists have historically positioned themselves in relationship to the larger movement for racial justice.[18]

For example, Badu's performance at the Sugar Water Festival on Saturday, July 30, 2005, in Columbus, Ohio, illustrates her

strong support of black men and the African American community.[19] During her performance, she decided to sing one of her
famous ballads. It is not uncommon for artists to focus on one
person in the audience when singing a ballad. As Badu started
to sing, a black man in the audience approached the stage, and
it appeared as if she was fine with this as she continued to look
in his direction as she sang. However, before the man could get
close enough to the stage, a member of the security staff, who
was white, stepped between the two of them. Badu stopped
singing and questioned the actions of the security guard. After
explaining that the security guard had ruined the mood, she
decided not to finish the song and moved on to the next song.
The crowd enthusiastically applauded this gesture. This move
on Badu's part was a clear signal that she feels a strong connection to black men and African Americans in general and that she
resented the suggestion that one of her fans, particularly a black
man, would be a threat to her safety. Despite the fact that there
are real threats that a celebrity can face in the midst of zealous
fans, Badu refused to be separated from her people and have the
love song that she was about to sing to this black man be interrupted by a white man.

Badu's "stand by your man" approach is not without excep-
tions. For example, in her song "Tyrone," she sings to a lover
who clearly is not meeting her needs and who in fact uses her
to take care of him.[20] The female protagonist in this song tells
her lover that he had "better call Tyrone to help him come and
get [his] shit." In other words, she is fed up with the numerous
excuses that this man gives her for his lack of attention and is
determined to not allow him to continue to use her financially
and sexually. This song became an anthem for Badu's female
fans. On her live album, which was released in 1997, you can hear
the enthusiasm of the women in the audience when Badu sings
the last line of the song: "I think you better call Tyrone, but you
can't use my phone." In Badu's narrative, African American men
deserve to have the support of African American women, but

that support does not include a license to abuse or take advantage of them. Badu's approach is similar to the ways that early blues singers complained about "no good men"[21] and contemporary rhythm and blues singers, such as Aretha Franklin, clamored for the respect of their men.[22] Badu's explicit critique of a black masculinity that harms African American women continues to resonate with her female fans.

Ndegéocello's celebration of black love is also linked to a critique of the experience of African American people in an oppressive, white, racist, and capitalist system. She indicts a racist capitalist system for creating the conditions of poverty and despair that are faced by members of poor urban communities. In addition, she identifies the racist capitalist system as a major precipitating factor in the incidence of drug addiction within the black community. In "Shoot'n Up and Gett'n High," she proclaims that there is a "capitalistic hand around [her] throat / Shoot'n up dope to cope in this dehumanizing society / We both found God when he O.D.'d."[23] Ndegéocello admits that she is having conversations with herself in her music but denies that her work is strictly autobiographical. She explains that "Shoot'n' Up and Gett'n High" is about a friend who despite his Harvard education is addicted to heroin.[24]

Reaching into the past to reclaim visual images and rhetoric of revolution is a way of raising consciousness and rejecting attempts to control the powerful black woman through stereotypes. Ndegéocello and Badu look to the past for guidance as they try to raise a revolutionary consciousness that emphasizes the centrality of African American women in the overall struggle for black civil rights. A closer look at the work of each of these artists reveals the ways that African American female artists negotiate black nationalism with a feminist sensibility as they seek to use their music and performances to support civil rights struggles.

Badu's concern with female empowerment and respect is reflected in the music video for her single "On & On,"[25] which she codirected with Paul Hunter. Her decision to use the film adaptation of Alice Walker's *The Color Purple* as inspiration further emphasizes the important bridge that Walker's work has served for young black women like Badu. The video begins with Badu walking through a field toward a house as she sings her freestyle single "Afro," which is featured on her first album. The song reminds her boyfriend or "daddy" to pick his Afro because it is flat on one side. This is one way that she interjects her Afrocentric sensibility into her interpretation of the film.

In the opening scene of the video, Badu's hair is wrapped. She sings and walks to the family house to hang laundry and do other domestic duties. She assumes the role of Celie in this portion of the video, but her narrative diverts considerably from both the book and filmic versions of *The Color Purple*. First, Badu is not married to an abusive husband and is connected to a larger family. As she climbs the stairs to the family home, her parents and her sister are leaving dressed in their finest clothes. As she walks toward them, her mother reminds her to do her chores and her sister sticks her tongue out at her. This is reminiscent of the classic narrative of Cinderella, who is forced to handle the domestic duties while her sisters live a lavish life. As she looks inside the house at the chaotic mess, she goes in and slams the door and the music to the video begins. As Badu walks around doing her various tasks, she sings,

> Oh, my, my, my / I'm feelin' high. My money's gone / I'm all alone / Too much to see, the world keeps turnin' / Oh what a day what a day / Peace and blessins' manifest / With every lesson learned / If your knowledge were your wealth / Then it would be well earned / If we were made in His image / Then call us by our names / Most intellects do not believe in God / But they fear us just the same.[26]

While Badu is left to care for the children and do the chores, the camera follows her as she moves from chore to chore with ease. This suggests a freedom that Walker's character, Celie, never had in either the book or the film. Badu handles each task easily and even stops to smell the flowers. There are also several moments of comic relief in the video. While chasing the dog, who has taken the wash from the line outside, Badu falls over a block of hay and lands in mud. She looks into a camera and proceeds to roll in the mud while singing her song. She falls back and relaxes in the mud, making a clear connection with the earth. The camera is positioned above her as she continues to sing. She relaxes and enjoys the feeling of the mud and then she heads back to the house. At the house, she sits in front of a mirror and surveys the damage to her clothes. The camera shoots her from behind and captures her reflection in the mirror as she contemplates what to do next. She looks at the emerald green tablecloth and back at the camera.

The next scene opens with Badu singing in the local juke joint. She has transformed into her version of Walker's character, Shug Avery. She is dressed in the tablecloth that she has fashioned into an African gown and has also used part of the cloth to wrap her hair in a traditional head wrap. She stands proudly among the members of the audience, who are tapping their feet and enjoying her performance. She sings,

> I'm feelin' kind of hungry / Cause my high is comin' down / Don't feed me yours / Cause your food does not endure / I think I need a cup of tea / The world keeps burnin' / Oh what a day, what a day, what a day.[27]

This scene lacks much of the raw sexuality that is depicted in the filmic adaptation of The Color Purple (1985). In the film, Shug Avery exudes sexuality and dances provocatively in her red dress, as the men sweat and drool over her. She thrusts her hips and shakes her breasts with pride and pleasure. In contrast, Badu stands like a queen imparting knowledge to her subjects who are clearly attentive, but not in a sexual way.[28] In addition to being a rejection of the oversexualized image of black women in music videos, this scene reaffirms her belief that black women are queens who deserve respect.

Several examples of Badu's use of the visual iconography have been featured on her official website.[29] For example, in a

FIGURE 5.2
Drawing on Erykah Badu's Website

bold drawing that appears on the site, she has blue skin (figure 5.2). The artistic choice to use blue skin rather than brown or black skin is interesting given Badu's emphasis on black pride. Perhaps she feels like an alien in the world we live in, or maybe she is suggesting some kind of evolved state of being that goes beyond the binaries of black and white. She is a cyborg, part human, part machine. This is very different from earlier images of Badu that seemed to emphasize an organic connection with the natural world.

This futuristic image of Badu conjures up dangerous notions of the wild, aggressive, and erotic black woman. Her legs are open and she leans seductively to the side. Her gaze is straight ahead and her expression is one of confidence. In addition to the blue skin, her hair sticks out in a mane of medusa-like spirals, conveying a wildness, danger, and freedom. The background is a series of bright red circles that spiral out like the speakers that are distributed around key parts of Badu's body, covering her breasts, stomach, and inner thighs. The largest circle covers her stomach, which emphasizes the role of reproduction as an important part of the revolutionary struggle.[30] Badu makes a clear connection between giving birth and her process of making music. For example, the cover art for her second album, *Erykah Badu: Live* (1997), includes a picture of Badu's exposed pregnant belly. Badu openly discussed and celebrated her first pregnancy and often used reproductive metaphors to describe her creative process. In an April 1997 interview with Deborah Gregory featured in *Essence*, Badu proclaims, "I'm a child of hip-hop raised on Stevie, Dinah, and Miles. Music is in labor now, and I'm a midwife helping with the delivery."[31] She considers herself and other new, young R&B singers as part of the rebirth of soul music. In addition, "mothering" within the context of Badu's work is accomplished through the passing on of warnings or advice given to her by the women who raised her. Badu gives advice on choosing one's friends in her song "Apple Tree," featured on her first album. In an interview with John Morthland, she explains that her grandmother was always "putting proverbs" on her. "One of 'em is you pick your friends like you pick your fruit, cause you don't want no rotten fruit."[32] She also warns African American women about carrying emotional baggage and burdens in

her popular song "Bag Lady," featured on her album *Mama's Gun* **99**
(2000).[33] In this way Badu plays the role of the wise woman who
passes on important lessons to younger generations.

In addition to emphasizing reproduction, the cyborg image
also embraces an explicit celebration of female sexuality and
freedom. The fact that this image is depicted on the website
for her recording company Control Freaq Records is significant
because it affirms the right of women to sexual agency and control. Badu reclaims black female sexual agency when she uses

the term *controlfreaq*. Within
male-dominated hip-hop culture, the term *freak* is often
used to demean women and
connotes a woman who is willing to do anything to please
her man.[34] Badu changes the
phrase and makes it clear that
she is in control and comfortable with her sexuality. This
picture is particularly interesting when compared to

FIGURE 5.3
*Drawing of Erykah Badu
with a Black Power Fist*

100   another image that was once prominently displayed on Badu's website. This drawing is of a closed fist raised in the black power salute. The major difference is that the thumbnail of this hand is painted bright red, which clearly identifies it with femininity. While affirming black nationalist politics, Badu embeds this image with a feminist sensibility that refocuses the attention back on the vast numbers of African American women who were crucial to the development, progress, and longevity of black civil rights groups at the height of the black power movement.[35] This produced a dilemma whereby performers like Badu negotiated their own needs to express their sexual agency among dominant stereotypes about the promiscuity of black women that have been reinforced by the commercial success of music with explicit lyrics and objectified images of black women's bodies in music videos.

Ndegéocello addresses this dilemma in a 2007 interview with honeysoul.com. When asked "What is your opinion of the music industry right now?" she responds, "I try not to have one. At its best, it's an illusion. At its worst, it's hard to stay motivated."[36] In a 2009 interview for *Pop Matters* magazine, she discusses her decision to simultaneously resist and maintain her commitment to the music. She explains,

> It is not for me to try to please other people, but to be true and honest and good with myself. Especially in the music industry, it's like people change themselves almost in the sense of creating mental anguish in order to make other people happy and to obtain celebrity and fame. . . . Some people do anything for their big dreams of sunshine.[37]

Counting herself among those who once strove for acceptance, Ndegéocello proudly announces that she's "no longer in that place." She explains, "I have tried to make people happy at my expense and I just don't do that anymore."[38] Her position challenges the notion that black women should be supportive helpmates or "fierce angels" who sacrifice themselves for the good of the community.[39]

Ndegéocello's concern with the illusory nature of the music business is captured in the video for her single "Pocketbook," released in 2002 on her album *Cookie: The Anthropological Mixtape*.[40] In this video, Ndegéocello shows how the drive to sell records and make money has become a defining feature of mainstream hip-hop and R&B. She does this as she dons the identity of a rapper (typically male) who is flocked by adoring fans in a nightclub. While men and women (not just women, which is typical of popular representations of video models)—dance around and enjoy themselves, Ndegéocello tells a story, but the story is not the typical misogyny-laced tale that privileges male conquest. Instead, she tells the story from the perspective of the video vixen (video model) who is simultaneously celebrated and reviled in mainstream culture. "Pocketbook" functions as an anthem that celebrates the agency of young women who use "the power of the p" to maintain a certain style of living. In the chorus to this song she says,

> she likes to have money in her pocketbook / and that's alright
> got a lot of sense runnin' through your bones / and that's alright.[41]

In this statement she not only speaks to those who would berate the choices of these women and categorize them as gold diggers but also speaks directly to the women both acknowledging their intelligence and affirming their right to have money that was earned "shaking their thangs." In this case "the masculinist performance" in which Ndegéocello engages is strategically used to promote a different narrative about the women who choose video modeling as a profession.[42] She also clearly identifies the ways that sex and women's bodies are used to sell products and records. She makes this explicit through her strategic use of product placement in her own video. As she sits on a throne, usually reserved for male performers, she forces the viewer to see that this performance can give us no real insight into the lives and psyches of these women. As we watch the dancers marked with the words "buy my record," we are forced to redirect our attention to the commercial interests that account

102   for the proliferation of these overly sexualized images of black womanhood.

Ndegéocello has contributed to the visual articulation of black revolutionary iconography through her star persona as well as through various albums that analyze oppression based on gender, race, class, and sexual orientation. Several of her singles integrate speeches by black feminists, such as Angela Davis and June Jordan, into songs that position Ndegéocello as "a revolutionary soul singer."[43] Her performances in music videos represent complex depictions of black female sexuality that reject strict binaries of male and female, gay and straight. This is accomplished through various techniques, but it is through her aesthetic choices that Ndegéocello occupies a liminal space that blurs the lines between masculine and feminine, gay and straight, identity politics and a more postmodern political sensibility. Through lyrics and performance, she uses her work to negotiate gender and sexual binaries. According to Judith Halberstam,

> Identity, it seems, as a representational strategy produces both power and danger; it provides both an obstacle to identification and a site "of necessary." As such, the stereotype, the image that announces identity in excess, is necessarily troublesome to an articulation of lesbian identity, but also foundational; the butch stereotype, furthermore, both makes lesbianism visible and yet seems to make it visible in non-lesbian terms: that is to say, the butch makes lesbianism readable in the register of masculinity, and it actually collaborates with the mainstream notion that lesbians cannot be feminine.[44]

Butch-femme culture among black lesbians has a long history that continues among young black lesbians today. In the January 2003 issue of *Vibe*, Kathy Dobie briefly chronicles the experiences of several young black lesbians who use the term *Aggressives* to refer to their expressions of butchness. "[B]utch means strapping down your chest, chopping off your hair, looking mannish. These girls want to look fly. The Aggressive persona is urban, hip, stylish, and bold.... On city streets aggression is a good thing, the word has a positive, macho ring, and no one hoots the word at you from a car window."[45] The fact that Dobie's exposé is featured in a magazine that covers the latest trends in hip-hop fashion and musical culture is important because it further highlights one of the ways that the black masculinity promoted in mainstream hip-hop culture is linked to modern performances of butchness by young black women.[46] In the case of Me'shell Ndegéocello, her performance of butchness signifies black bisexuality by referencing a specific type of black masculinity, which is closely associated with young black men. However, this is not to suggest that this performance of black masculinity is uniquely male, only that it draws on behaviors and gestures associated with black men in the popular media. Ndegéocello's embodiment of a black queer aesthetic comments on black masculinity while simultaneously performing a version of black female sexuality that resists a strictly heteronormative narrative of sexual identity and expression.[47]

For example, in the video for her hit single "If That's Your Boyfriend (He Wasn't Last Night)," she takes a song that emphasizes competition between women for the attention of men and imposes a visual narrative that unites women through the visible pain experienced by the women in the video. While the song positions Ndegéocello as a cold-hearted woman who would willingly sleep with another woman's man, it also reveals a complex image of how self-hatred among women can threaten female solidarity. This is consistent with Ndegéocello's description of her early work as "love poems in the middle of revolution."[48] She further explains in an interview in Harper's Bazaar that many of her songs are based on personal experiences as a black, bisexual woman.[49] She was labeled a misogynist for her song "If That's Your Boyfriend," but she explains that this song emerged from a very painful experience in her life:

> I met this guy once, and most of the girls said there was no way he could like me because of the way I looked. There's an amazing misogyny among women, and I wanted to write about it.[50]

This may explain why her video for the song features women, all of whom are suffering from rejection, low self-esteem, or insecurity. As a result, the visual images in the video highlight women's position and their complicity in a misogynist society. They also highlight the pain and confusion caused by rejection.

Shot in black and white, the video opens with a close-up shot of a light-skinned African American woman with curly short hair, who, with closed eyes, says, "Roaming among the rubble of hate, field hand hair and master's face didn't stop me from meeting the noose." This statement emphasizes the reality of skin color privilege among African Americans while simultaneously rejecting it as a form of protection against racial hatred and violence. Beginning with a reference to slavery, skin color, and lynching is strategic here because it emphasizes the inextricable ways that race, class, gender, and sexuality converge in an oppressive society. Through her use of this opening monologue, Ndegéocello signals to the audience that they are not about to see a "cat fight," but instead something much deeper.

After the opening monologue, the camera moves to a shot of Me'shell with her head down pounding the first few notes of the song on the piano. The video features women of various ages and ethnicities who speak throughout the video. They have short hair, long hair, braids, natural hair, or straightened hair, and at least one is bald. Some of the women wear makeup, some do not. In the video, each woman expresses her honest outrage, sadness, and rage about infidelity and her individual approach to relationships. Close-up shots of each woman emphasize the importance of each woman's feelings. This contrasts with the female betrayal and lack of caring that is emphasized in the lyrics of the song. The video does not present an overwhelming narrative of female solidarity or unity. However, there is a consistent exploration of the multiple ways that external and internalized oppression harm various women. The only men in the video are two members of Ndegéocello's band who sporadically appear throughout the video.

In addition to the centrality of women's experience from a variety of perspectives, Me'shell Ndegéocello's performance of masculinity and femininity reflects the revolutionary way that her work negotiates binary oppositions. She simultaneously affirms the performance of butch lesbian identity and femininity in her physical appearance. She has a bald head, but she wears a full face of makeup. Most striking is the heavy and shiny lipstick that she wears. She also has on a men's A-line tank top, and her baggy slacks are supported by suspenders. As she plays her bass and sings the song, she confidently dances and sings, unapologetically affirming her decision to sleep with another woman's man.

While the song is clearly about having sex with a man, shot-reverse-shot is used to affirm lesbian desire. In the bridge to the song, Ndegéocello stops playing her bass and dances seductively as she sings the following:

> Ooh ooh, baby baby / good to the last lick at the bottom of the bag and / ooh, baby baby, make you wanna do things that you never have / ooh baby / mad sex / and when we're through / I really have no problem actin' like I don't know you.[51]

During this section of the video, her lyrics are briefly interrupted by one of the black women featured in the video. After Ndegéocello sings "mad sex," the camera moves to this woman, who responds, "Who is she?" The camera then immediately goes back to Ndegéocello, who says, "And when we're through." The camera goes back to the woman, who says, "What?"

Through the use of shot-reverse-shot, it appears as if Ndegéocello is singing to this woman. This is one of the only depictions of a visual and lyrical interaction between women in the video. This scene is also significant because it suggests butch-femme desire. The woman is stereotypically feminine in terms of her dress and overall look, which is contrasted to Ndegéocello's performance of butchness in this portion of the video. Consequently, the lyrics and the camera allow an expression of queer identity to emerge within a song that is about sex with a man. In this way, Ndegéocello's revolutionary performance of black queerness forces her audience to move outside comfortable categories of gay and straight, male and female, black and white.

Me'shell Ndegéocello and Erykah Badu are examples of artists who despite the status of African American women within hip-hop culture have reclaimed a sense of agency and subjectivity as women, while simultaneously raising awareness about the needs of the entire African American community. Their works explore their inner psyches and the complexities of being black women in a world that often marginalizes and excludes the perspectives of black women. Both artists use their music and performances to theorize and define a revolutionary agenda that affirms the entire black community. This is accomplished through strategies that focus on self-definition and naming, embracing a black aesthetic, asserting women's sexual agency, and confronting oppression in all its forms.

6

THE MANY IMAGES OF THE REVOLUTIONARY BLACK WOMAN
Michelle Obama Reconsidered

America's first lady, Mrs. Michelle Obama, the most prominent woman in the country, has double roles to negotiate. She is responsible for the usual duties incumbent upon the first lady, but because of her race, she also must contend with and react to the stereotypical images of strong black women. Representations of Michelle Obama, as well as the rhetoric surrounding her husband's campaign and his first term as president of the United States, illustrate the persistence of visual images that reinforce perceptions of revolutionary black women as dangerous and un-American. In the eyes of much of the public in the United States, a black female revolutionary can be summed up in one image: a black woman with a big Afro, a gun, and an attitude to match. She is considered a danger to our nation and a threat to political power. For many, she stands as a symbol of blackness and femaleness gone mad, both of which need to be curbed. Although the image of the black female revolutionary is very specific, it gets applied to a broad range of black women—professional and working-class women in an effort to depict them as examples of out of control blackness and femaleness that threaten the "American" way of life. This discourse about American values is often code for white, male, heterosexual,

Anglo-Saxon Protestant values. As with anything, this powerful image can be mediated, but even the ways that it can be mediated reveal the power of racialized and gendered images and the power they hold over people's actions and presentation in public. The popular image of the dangerous, unpatriotic black female revolutionary was utilized against Michelle Obama during her husband's campaign for president in 2008. However, there are numerous ways that she and her supporters have used other images to negate this past perception of her as a black revolutionary and recast her in three major roles—"Mom in Chief," "Fashion Icon," and "Just One of the Girls."

The negative representation of Michelle Obama began when her husband announced his plans to run for president. Members of the right-wing media depicted her as a dangerous and radical black woman, one who was orchestrating the various moves of Barack Obama. During the campaign, Michelle Obama was a very different person than she is now.[1] She was a central and active part of her husband's campaign. She wrote her own speeches, in which she spoke confidently about her experiences as a working-class African American woman who worked her way through Princeton and Harvard and became a successful attorney. She emphasized the importance of American values and the opportunities that made this possible for her and her husband. During the campaign, Mrs. Obama was very vocal about political issues and the direction that she and her husband wanted to take our country.

In fact, when Barack and Michelle Obama were interviewed before the 2008 election, Mr. Obama made his wife's role quite clear. When asked whether he would consider giving his wife a position if he became president, he said, "Well, look. Michelle is one of the smartest people that I know. She is my chief counsel and adviser. I would never make a big decision without asking her opinion."[2] It is telling that when the interviewer asked the question, Michelle purportedly whispered in Barack's ear, "Say no." And when he deferred to her, she responded, "No, no" and proceeded to discuss her top priority, her two children.[3] This was a considerable shift from the more vocal role that she played earlier in the campaign. After one of her most famous speeches in February of 2008, Mrs. Obama received extensive coverage and attacks from opponents because of the following statement:

> What we have learned over this year is that hope is making a comeback. It is making a comeback. And let me tell you something—for the first time in my adult lifetime, I am really proud of my country. And not just because Barack has done well, but because I think people are hungry for change. And I have been desperate to see our country moving in that direction and just not feeling so alone in my frustration and disappointment. I've seen people who are hungry to be unified around some basic common issues, and it's made me proud.[4]

Critics rushed to label Mrs. Obama as an angry black woman, whose lack of patriotism disqualified her husband from being the next president of the United States.[5] In the minds of some, her comments positioned her squarely within the popular image of the angry black woman. In fact, during a *Fox News Watch* report on Michelle Obama and the media,[6] conservative and liberal commentators discussed media reactions to Mrs. Obama and the implications for her husband's campaign.[7] During this discussion commentators were surprisingly candid about the ways that the portrayal of Michelle Obama as an angry black woman would affect her husband's campaign. One of the featured commentators, Jane Hall of American University, discussed the strategy of "othering" Barack Obama in order to defeat him. She argued that those using this strategy reasoned, "If we can't prove he's Muslim, then let's prove that his wife is an angry black woman."[8] The following exchange ensued:

> *Thomas:* I want to pick up on something that Jane said about the angry black woman. Look at the image of angry black women on television. Politically you have Maxine Waters of California, liberal Democrat. She's always angry every time she gets on television. Cynthia McKinney, another angry black woman. And who are

the black women you see on the local news at night in
cities all over the country. They're usually angry about
something. They've had a son who has been shot in a
drive-by shooting. They are angry at Bush. So you don't
really have a profile of non-angry black women.
[*Crosstalk*]
Pinkerton: Oprah Winfrey.
Thomas: Oprah Winfrey. Yes, there you go, Oprah Winfrey.
Hall: I wasn't endorsing that concept [but] that some people
are going to go after her.

The ease with which Cal Thomas asserts that all of the prominent
African American women on television are angry is evidence that
the stereotype of the angry black woman is still firmly entrenched
in American popular culture. It also shows that any black woman
who speaks up in public about injustice can have her credibility
diminished simply by calling her angry.[9] According to Thomas,
the only black woman on television who is not angry is Oprah
Winfrey.[10] The juxtaposition of Oprah and all these other suppos-
edly angry black women is an important point that I will consider later as part of my discussion of Winfrey's public support of
Barack and Michelle Obama.

The growing discourses that cast Mrs. Obama in the role
of the powerful stereotypical image of the angry black woman
would find itself embodied in the July 21, 2008, cover of *The
New Yorker* (figure 6.1). A close reading of *The New Yorker* cover
that features caricatures of President Obama and Mrs. Obama,
titled "The Politics of Fear," by *New Yorker* illustrator Barry Blitt,
reveals how even the most powerful African American woman
in the country is not immune from sexist and racist attitudes
that result in the construction of black women as domineering,
angry, unpatriotic, militant, and dangerous. The cover depicts
Mrs. Obama as a gun-toting, Afro-wearing terrorist and reveals
the power of the black revolutionary female stereotype to the
American cultural landscape since the seventies. While the editors meant this picture to be a satire on the very stereotypical

images that it represents and a critique of the way fear tactics 111
were being used to malign the Obamas, the fact remains that it
contains visual elements that depend on an implicit understanding of a stereotypical militancy among African American women
that often gets coded in the popular media.

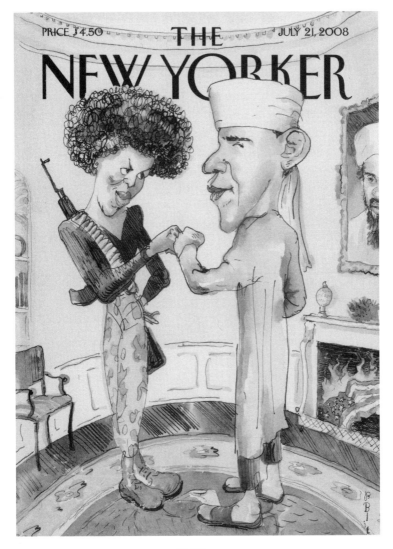

FIGURE 6.1
Drawing of the Obamas on the July 21, 2008, Cover of The New Yorker

Mrs. Obama is depicted with menacing eyes that stare intently into the eyes of her husband. Her eyes have a hypnotic quality to them that reinforces this construction of her as the most important African American woman in the world. Her look says, "We did it! We fooled them into electing you, now time for the real fun." The couple stands in an oval-shaped room on a rug that bears the federal seal. It should also be noted that Barack steps on the neck of the bald eagle, an important symbol of freedom for which the United States stands. The room contains a portrait of Osama bin Laden, which mirrors the caricature of Barack Obama dressed in traditional Islamic garb. This portrait is directly above an American flag burning in the fireplace below. Michelle has a sly grin on her face that suggests a hidden and devious agenda, and the gun, fatigues, and natural hairstyle all conjure images of revolutionary black women from the seventies. Her grin also signifies a devious, calculating state of mind and, when paired with the goofy grin that her husband wears, suggests that she is the real brains behind this caricatured representation of the couple. In this depiction she is clearly in charge. She embodies a uniquely American construction of black women as militant troublemakers.[11] The robe that Obama wears emphasizes his perceived foreignness and reinforces the ridiculous idea that he is an undercover Muslim,[12] who cannot really prove that he was born in the United States. There have been numerous challenges, under the guise of the birther movement, to the Obama presidency based on the false belief that he was not born in the United States. Donald Trump was one of its most powerful members. These stereotypical images of the Obamas, along with the American flag burning in the oval office fire and the bald eagle choking under the weight of Obama's foot, depict a cultural nightmare that sees the success of this powerful couple as a real threat to American prosperity and way of life.

The Afro in this cartoon is an important device that links Michelle Obama to the stereotypical militant black woman that emerged in representations of revolutionary African American women in the 1970s, such as Angela Davis and Kathleen Cleaver. While there have always been black women who have worn their hair in its natural state, the association of the Afro hairstyle with black nationalist politics was an important part of the growing militancy of the fight of black people for civil rights in the late sixties and seventies. Because of this history, this hairstyle remains an important reference point within the American cultural context.[13] That prominent black women within politics have often been characterized as dangerous through the marker of hair is another important part of this discussion. Cal Thomas' mention of Congresswoman Cynthia McKinney referenced the incident that involved McKinney being escorted off federal property and later arrested for assaulting a security officer when she refused to show identification because the guard did not recognize her with a new hairdo.[14] This new hairdo featured McKinney's hair in its natural state, unencumbered by a bun or some other device to keep it controlled. McKinney's experience shows the way that visual markers of black female beauty and expression are interpreted and galvanized to justify the false assumption that black women are a threat to core American values and ideals. The "untamed hair" thus becomes a signifier for an untamed political identity.[15]

In addition to the clothing and hairstyle, the "fist bump" is prominently figured in The New Yorker cover. On the night that Barack Obama won the Democratic nomination, he and Mrs. Obama hugged and gently bumped fists.[16] Writing for the Washington Post, Amy Argetsinger and Roxanne Roberts referred to it as "the fist bump heard 'round the world."[17] This simple expression of congratulation and love received an unusual amount of attention from the media.[18] Because this famous fist bump, a gesture associated with black urban life,[19] made its appearance in such a public way, in an arena where one would not expect to see it, there was quite a bit of speculation about what this could tell us about this young couple, who might become the first African American president and first lady. This very culturally specific expression of support, celebration, and love by this successful African American couple for some represented an authentic expression of black identity that confirmed that the Obamas were real, everyday black folks and for others represented another piece of evidence that the Obamas could not be trusted. The fascination and frequency with which the mass media wrote about this innocent and touching expression of love, solidarity, and much-deserved celebration of achievement suggests cultural anxieties about race that were being projected on this couple. This "we did it moment" in many ways should be no more remarkable than teammates congratulating one another following a big win. However, because of the anxieties about race in this country and the uneasiness with which some Americans viewed this young African American man and his family, the fist bump became a problem in the imagination of the country.[20] This very public use of a very culturally specific gesture, at a point when many people said that Obama's election meant "that race no longer mattered," on a deep level manifested the deep anxieties that some Americans have about dealing with "real black people." The use of the angry black woman stereotype, along with other strategies designed to derail Barack Obama's candidacy, failed. However, the stereotypes that emerged during the campaign remained relevant in the numerous ways that the first lady managed her image once Obama took office.

Michelle Obama's role as advisor and confidant to her husband is a source of concern for many who are afraid that she will not remain in her proper place as first lady. Her proximity to the "leader of the free world" positions her where she can be easily scrutinized and targeted for accusations. In many ways, she is not unlike other outspoken first ladies such as Nancy Reagan and Hillary Clinton, who at various points in their husbands' presidencies were accused of trying to run the country through their respective marital relationships. This fear of a woman covertly running the nation is symptomatic of a larger resistance on the part of the American electorate to consider a woman for president because of cultural myths about the inability of women to be confident and forceful leaders. Mrs. Obama is aware of this concern and tries to emphasize her role as a helpmate to her husband rather than a person whom he consults for political or policy advice. In an article in the March 9, 2009, issue of *People*, she makes a point of emphasizing that he does not consult her on policy matters and that the last thing that he consulted her on was spring break. In addition, the author makes a point of assuring the reader that the president's aides have confirmed that it has never been Mrs. Obama's "style to weigh in at his policymaking table."[21] The emphasis that is placed on defining Michelle Obama as a helpmate to her husband works to diminish any concerns that she is in any way controlling the White House agenda and counters the militant caricature of her in *The New Yorker*.

Being the first African American woman in the role of first lady exposes Mrs. Obama to a kind of scrutiny that is gendered, raced, and classed. That is, her status as an African American woman who grew up on the South Side of Chicago brings with it a variety of discourses about black womanhood and its relationship to the nation-state. The image of the predominately black and Hispanic South Side of Chicago, which has been historically represented in the mainstream imagination as the embodiment of violence, crime, and poverty, is an important referent that links Mrs. Obama to the black underclass. Many of the women of color who inhabit the South Side are stereotyped as welfare queens who are more interested in watching television and collecting a government check than raising their children. This image became an important part of the American discourse when President Reagan discussed the cheating of the welfare system by black women on the South Side of Chicago.[22] This is one of the numerous ways that black women have been stereotyped as lazy, bad mothers who have more children in order to collect money.[23] Another important stereotype that is associated with welfare mothers is the term "baby mama."[24] This is a common term used to describe someone with whom a man has a child. The term has negative connotations in that these women are seen as troublemakers who make the lives of their "baby's daddy" miserable, also known as "baby mama drama." In his June 11, 2008, column on Salon.com, Alex Koppelman reported that a Fox News commentator referred to Michelle Obama as "Barack Obama's Baby Mama."[25] Mrs. Obama's decision to construct her public persona as "Mother in Chief" provides an important contrasting image to the stereotypical images of the welfare queen and baby mama.

Michelle Obama's first one hundred days as first lady were as much about responding to negative perceptions (promoted by opponents of the Obama–Biden ticket) of her as an angry unpatriotic black woman who would have a tremendous and detrimental influence on the path of the country as they were about a particular national agenda. Through her focus on her roles as a wife and mother to both her family and the nation, Michelle Obama successfully shifted attention away from any potential threat that she may pose as an important player in White House politics. The emphasis on traditional gender roles and her focus on nurturing helped to temporarily shield her from the type of ridicule directed at Hillary Clinton when she went beyond the traditional role of the first lady and took on health care reform. Popular discourse about Michelle Obama's role as Mom in Chief both reinforces accepted gender expectations for all women and makes it possible for a new, more positive perception of black mothers to emerge in the national consciousness. In addition, her commitment to supporting military families, nurturing her children, and providing support for local communities, and her dedication to making the White House more open to citizens, are part of a carefully designed strategy to counter negative portrayals of her as unpatriotic that emerged during her husband's campaign in 2008.

Allison Samuels' feature article in the December 1, 2008, issue of *Newsweek*, "What Michelle Means to Us," argues that having Michelle as "the new Mom in Chief" could do much to explode stereotypes about black women.[26] Michelle Obama is also very aware of the ways that black women and girls are looking at her as a role model. In an interview for *People*, she says that one of the reasons that she decided to put on a designer dress and pose for *Vogue* was because she believes that it "was good for [her] daughters and little girls just like them, who haven't seen themselves represented in these magazines, hopefully to talk more broadly about what beauty is, what intelligence is, what counts."[27] African American women had lots of hope that somehow having a black woman in this prominent position would force mainstream America to reconsider their false assumptions about black women. Samuels cites an exchange on the *Tom Joyner Show*, a popular radio program in the African American community, in which he asked black women whether Obama's choice of a wife impacted their decision to vote for him. One woman said, "She's a regular sister," and "I love the fact that she looks like the woman next door or like my cousin or niece."[28] The fact that Michelle is "real," defined as down-to-earth and approachable, and is an African American woman who has dark skin is important because it highlights the extent to which skin color privilege remains an important factor in the construction of black women. Embracing the role of "Mom in Chief" on the one hand challenges the stereotypical image of black matriarchs who emasculate black men and who are blamed for the failure of black families to rise out of poverty.[29] On the other hand, this emphasis on domesticity and nurturance of the nation in many ways caters to an American mainstream that was raised on images of the stereotypical mammy: the dedicated, dark-skinned domestic servant.[30] Consequently, in her attempt to claim a legitimate space for herself as first lady, Michelle Obama is caught between two controlling images of black womanhood,[31] which affect the choices that she can make in the public sphere.[32]

The intense scrutiny of Obama's body and her fashion is another example of the ways that black women's bodies have

118

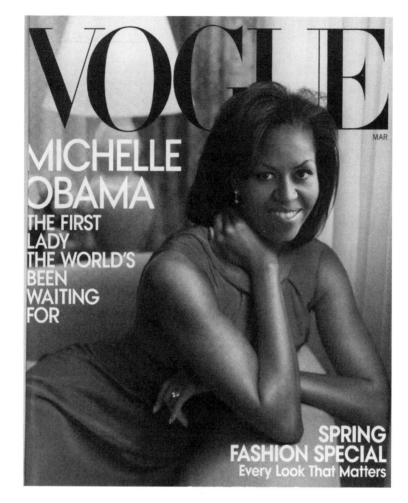

FIGURE 6.2
Michelle Obama on the March 2009 Issue of Vogue

always been subjected to surveillance and regulation.[33] In 2009 Mrs. Obama graced the cover of the March issue of *Vogue* (figure 6.2).[34] She insisted on wearing her own clothes and having her own hair stylist and makeup artist prepare her for the shoot.[35] The photograph depicts her leaning coyly against what appears to be a sofa or chair. The cover reads, "Michelle Obama: The First Lady the World's Been Waiting For." There is a seductive

FIGURE 6.3
The Official White House Portrait of Michelle Obama

element to the photograph that is very different from the official White House photograph that is featured on her website (figure 6.3). Both photographs are welcoming, emphasizing Mrs. Obama's smile and physical beauty. However, the seductiveness of the *Vogue* cover downplays the power that invariably comes with being the first lady of the United States. While the official White House photo invites the viewer in and features the domestic element of flowers, Mrs. Obama's stance is more erect and confident, not alluring or seductive. Rather than donning a suit, Mrs. Obama wears a little black dress and pearls, standard attire for the society woman ready to entertain. This is compatible with her presentation of herself as a proper lady, mother, and wife. However, her stance emphasizes her athletic build and thus her strength unlike the *Vogue* cover which despite her bare arms suggests a more guarded and demure performance of femininity. One could argue that the prominence of her buff physique and her confident stance in the photo appear masculine. However, other markers of femininity, that is, the little black dress, pearls, and flowers, work to mitigate the masculine nature of the stance. Consequently, while both photos invite the viewer into Mrs. Obama's world, the official White House photo portrays a more professional and business-oriented Michelle, while the lounging Michelle on the *Vogue* cover seductively invites the reader to join her on the sofa.

On the *Vogue* cover, directly beneath the lounging Michelle we see two phrases that sum up the tension inherent in the way we view the role of the first lady. The first caption reads "Spring Fashion Special: Every Look That Matters," and the second caption reads "Super Powers! Queen Rania of Jordan, Carla Bruni-Sarkozy, and Melinda Gates." The pairing of these tag statements makes a clear connection between beauty and power. The cover constructs all four women as important and powerful figures on the international stage, primarily because of their relationships with powerful men. This is important to an analysis of Michelle Obama because it serves to eclipse a very important part of her relationship to President Obama. She was and is his mentor. This part of their relationship began when he joined her law firm as a young attorney.

Later in the issue, fashion editor André Leon Talley begins his feature article on Michelle Obama with the following statement:

"From envisioning a more inclusive White House to embracing fearless fashion, Michelle Obama is poised to become the most transformative First Lady in history."[36] Of course, the emphasis on fashion is expected given the status of *Vogue* as one of the most important fashion magazines in the world. However, the focus on Mrs. Obama's fashion within the mainstream media, including venues not specifically concerned with fashion, downplays the significance of Mrs. Obama as a guiding political force in the career of her husband and the future of the nation. This is the reality that the cover of *Vogue* elides. The representation of Mrs. Obama as the seductive, lounging woman who is not just what "America has been waiting for" but also the docile, waiting woman who is poised to serve relegates her to a sexualized image too often used to depict women of color. This process of sexual objectification is one way of addressing cultural anxieties about angry black womanhood that characterized earlier reactions to Michelle Obama. This type of sexual objectification of black womanhood was apparent in the representations of black women, such as those of Angela Davis and Kathleen Cleaver, discussed earlier.

The appearance of Michelle Obama with Oprah Winfrey on the cover of *O* provides another important example of the ways that media representations of the first lady mediate the significance of Mrs. Obama as the first African American first lady. Oprah Winfrey is recognized as one of the most powerful black women in America.[37] Millions of American women, many of whom are white, have turned to Oprah for years. She has been someone to be trusted with all of their thoughts and fears. She told them how to cope. She cried with them. She laughed with them. She gave them cars! Michelle Obama's relationship with Oprah along with her appearance on daytime television shows like *The View* would go a long way in helping her to mediate the various stereotypes that plagued her earlier in her life as the wife of a career politician.

When Michelle Obama joined the ladies of the popular daytime television show *The View*, shortly after her husband won

122   the Democratic nomination for president, she began a process of cultivating an image of herself as just one of the girls. This aspect of her growing public persona was another example of the ways that she managed the negativity that she faced. During the opening segment Mrs. Obama joined Whoopi Goldberg, Joy Behar, Sherri Shepherd, Barbara Walters, and Elisabeth Hasselbeck as a cohost for the show.[38] Her willingness to host put her on the same level as the regular hosts and gave her an opportunity to show the public that she was like all the other women, that is, she has something to say about the most recent "hot topics," including everything from politics to the latest fashion trends.

As the group of women organize themselves at the large table on the set, Mrs. Obama smiles and says, "I have to be greeted properly. Fist bump please." She explains, "I got it from the young staff. That's the new high five." That she greeted each woman with a fist bump, a gesture that had received so much attention after she used it to congratulate her husband on winning the Democratic nomination, brought the common greeting among black males in the inner city into a very different context. It symbolized a type of bridge building between black and white women as well as an opportunity to change negative perspectives about her. Sharing this moment with Elisabeth Hasselbeck, the only outspoken conservative Republican on the show, produced a symbolic moment of the coming together of not only black and white women but also Republican and Democrat.

The "yes we can get along" narrative undergirding Michelle's gesture toward the other women extended an important aspect of Barack Obama's overall message of working together across differences. At this moment the fist bump was transformed from a specific type of cultural expression into a symbol of cross-cultural communication and civility despite racial, ethnic, cultural, and political differences. In fact, later in the show, when Matthew Broderick enters, he is greeted with either a handshake or a hug by Hasselbeck, Shepherd, and Obama. When he reaches out to Joy Behar, she extends her fist and says, "We do this now!"

At this moment in the broadcast, Behar easily appropriates this very specific cultural exchange associated with black men in the inner city into a gesture that upper-class white men and women can use to greet each other. Mrs. Obama's generous sharing of this cultural practice with these women functioned to lessen any cultural anxieties about the difference that the Obamas represented and further moved Michelle Obama away from the image of her as an angry black woman who hated America and white people and closer to being understood as a relatable, everyday woman.

But more than any other relationship, Michelle Obama's relationship with Oprah Winfrey went a long way in creating a new public persona for her that emphasized the ways that she was another American woman juggling the challenges of raising a family and her career as first lady of the United States. The April 2009 issue of Winfrey's O magazine features the two women strolling on the White House grounds in vibrantly colored spring dresses (figure 6.4). They appear to be having a relaxed conversation as they enjoy their surroundings. The headline reads, "Michelle Obama's Brand New Life" and tells the reader that the new first lady "opens her home and tells Oprah what's keeping her real (including Oval Office drop-ins and the joys of White House pie)."[39] Both the photo and the headline emphasize domesticity and American values and seek to construct Michelle Obama and her family as being as American as apple pie. This is a modern version of the way that Sojourner Truth used traditional markers of femininity in the construction of her image. This issue of the magazine features the first official interview that Mrs. Obama gave from the White House. This was also the first time that Oprah had ever shared the cover of her magazine with another person.[40] In her opening statement for the issue, Oprah introduces the new first lady to her readers in the following way:

Brilliant yet *sensible*, accomplished yet *down-to-earth*, tough yet surprisingly *softhearted*, Michelle is no stranger to shaking things up. From her candor on the campaign trail to her outspoken advocacy on behalf of working mothers and military families, this is a woman who has the courage of her convictions.[41]

Sharing the cover with Obama and offering a description of her that affirmed both her intelligence and her strength while simultaneously emphasizing how "sensible," "down-to-earth," and "surprising softhearted" she is set the stage for Michelle Obama to counteract early perceptions of her as an angry, unpatriotic,

FIGURE 6.4
Michelle Obama on the Cover of the April 2009 Issue of O

black woman. In the feature article of the issue, "Oprah Talks to Michelle Obama," Winfrey again emphasizes the ways in which the new first lady is relatable. She explains,

> Yet for all the majesty of the White House, the First Lady has already infused it with *a palpable ease*; her presence makes the place feel *open and approachable*. When we sit down to talk, she seems as *relaxed* as she did when I first interviewed her and her husband in their Chicago apartment in 2004.[42]

Next to the opening pages of this piece is another photo of the two women smiling playfully into the camera, as Michelle places her arm around Oprah and the two hold hands as they stand in the Jacqueline Kennedy Garden.[43] It is important that one of television's most beloved talk show hosts vouches for Mrs. Obama and her husband, making it possible for the new first lady to continue cultivating her image as the dutiful wife and mother who is committed to helping military families and promoting a healthy America through her emphasis on healthy eating and ending childhood obesity. When Oprah asks her how people address her when she visits the school that her daughter attends, Mrs. Obama responds,

> When I introduce myself, I usually say, "Hi, I'm Michelle—Malia and Sasha's mom." And then when you sit down with another parent and have a conversation, all the titles melt away anyway, and you are just talking about your kids.[44]

In this exchange, Obama emphasizes her identity as a mother and as an everyday woman. She goes on to discuss how she organizes her workday around getting the girls off to school and picking them up at the end of the day. She also emphasizes how living in the White House provides a type of normalcy that makes it easier for her family to share quality time. She says,

> That's the beauty of living above the office: Barack is home every day. The four of us sit down to eat as a family. We haven't had that kind of normalcy for years. And now I can just pop over to his office, which sometimes I'll do if I know he's having a particularly frustrating day.[45]

With this statement, Mrs. Obama deemphasizes the extraordinary aspects of being part of the first family. Instead, she emphasizes the ways that she and her family are just like other American families, except that she has the privilege to "pop over" to her husband's office to give him comfort when he's having a rough day. Throughout the interview with Oprah, she emphasizes that her new home belongs to America. She explains, "We feel privileged, and we feel a responsibility to make it feel like the people's house. We have the good fortune of being able to sleep here, but this house belongs to America." If any readers with anxieties about whether the Obamas were really radicals who would destroy America (remember the caricatures on *The New Yorker*) remained, Mrs. Obama's discussion with Oprah was designed to address them.

Despite Michelle Obama's excellent service to the nation, the January 2012 release of Jodi Kantor's purported tell-all book *The Obamas* created a political and journalistic firestorm and charges that Kantor's portrayal of the first lady is an unfair depiction that represents her as an angry black woman.[46] Once again, Mrs. Obama was confronted by this persistent stereotype. The initial coverage of the book constructed a battle between Jodi Kantor and Michelle Obama. The headlines generally used one of two narratives. Headlines like "Author Defends Michelle Portrait," "Jodi Kantor Refutes Michelle Obama's 'Angry Black Woman' Claim," and "Jodi Kantor Talks about White House Blowback on Her Book, *The Obamas*" focus on Kantor's response to criticism of her portrayal.[47] Conversely, reports about Michelle Obama focus on her denial that she is angry. Examples include "Michelle Obama Denies She Is an 'Angry Black Woman' in White House," "First Lady: Wrong to Paint Her as 'Angry Black Woman,'" and "Michelle Obama: People Have Tried to Paint Me as 'Some Angry Black Woman.'"[48] This constructed and sensationalized "catfight" is tangential to the main focus of *Iconic*. Rather than engage in an extensive study of Kantor's book, *Iconic* is concerned with an analysis of how Michelle Obama's initial response to the controversy provides another example of the strategies that revolutionary black women use to combat and transcend the stereotype of the angry black woman. In her highly publicized interview with Gayle King on CBS, Mrs. Obama discusses everything from the pictures in her office in the East Wing to how she manages the lives of her two daughters, Malia and Sasha. In the lengthy interview, King eventually asks about Mrs. Obama's reaction to Kantor's book, *The Obamas*. Mrs. Obama responds,

> I guess it's more interesting to imagine this conflicted situation here and a strong woman and—you know? But that's been an image that people have tried to paint of me since the day Barack announced [his candidacy], that I'm some angry black woman.[49]

She also denies claims that she had conflicts with former White House chief of staff Rahm Emanuel and former press secretary Robert Gibbs.[50] She also assures King that she has no intention of reading Kantor's book and explains, "[W]ho can write about how I feel? Who? What third person can tell me how I feel, or anybody for that matter?"[51] With this statement she claims a protective space that affirms her self-identity and blocks the intrusive attempts of others to define her. In this exchange, Mrs. Obama again resists any attempts to paint her as angry, unhappy, and difficult to work with.

Unlike the March 2009 interview in *People* in which she downplays her role as an advisor to her husband, in her interview with Gayle King she openly admits that she is one of her husband's "biggest confidantes." However, she adds that Barack "has dozens of smart people who surround him. . . . That's not to say that we don't have discussions and conversations. That's not to say that my husband doesn't know how I feel."[52] She also reveals that her husband has her ear. However, this minor admission is overshadowed by the amount of time that the first lady spends discussing her work with military families, her campaign to fight childhood obesity, her commitment to doing her job as first lady, and being there for her children and her husband as he seeks another term

128   in office. Even as she expresses her excitement about helping her husband's campaign, she carefully reinforces an image of herself as a mother and everyday working woman. She makes a gesture that invites others to get to know her. She says, "You know, I just try to be me. And my hope is that over time people get to know me. And they get to judge me for me."[53]

While Mrs. Obama's invitation for others to get to know her is an important gesture, like the other revolutionary women in this study she is still aware of the classic struggle against negative images that are deployed to control strong black women and thwart their goals for revolutionary change. Michelle Obama, Sojourner Truth, Angela Davis, Kathleen Cleaver, Pam Grier, Etang Inyang, Alice Walker, Audre Lorde, Erykah Badu, and Me'shell Ndegéocello use complex strategies to transcend negativity and focus their energy on their own agendas. The result is the presence of African American women who contribute to societal change through resisting negative images promoted by a society fearful of their power. Their knowledge of these stereotypes helps them to develop counterimages that support truths about themselves, which in turn helps them to push forward in their quests to promote social justice and equality for all.

NOTES

CHAPTER 1

1   Graham is a regular contributor to *NewsBusters*, a conservative blog.
2   Tim Graham, "Larry King Kept Asking Michelle Obama: 'Attack Dog' Palin Doesn't Make You Mad?" *Newsbusters.org*, October 10, 2008, http://newsbusters.org/blogs/tim-graham/2008/10/10/larry-king-kept-asking-michelle-obama-attack-dog-palin-doesnt-make-you-m.
3   In "African-American Women's History and the Metalanguage of Race," *Signs* 17, no. 21 (1992): 251–73, Evelyn Brooks Higginbotham discusses the association of blacks by the American public with welfare and the drug problem (254). See also Michael Omi and Howard Winant's *Racial Formation in the United States from the 1960s to the 1980s* (New York: Routledge & Kegan Paul, 1986), as well as Jesse Carney Smith's *Images of Blacks in American Culture: A Reference Guide to Information Sources* (Westport, Conn.: Greenwood Press, 1988).
4   Recall the dismissal of Anita Hill's claim that U.S. Supreme Court nominee Clarence Thomas had sexually harassed her. Thomas and his supporters claimed that Hill was an angry woman scorned. See Toni Morrison's collection of essays, *Race-ing Justice, En-gendering Power: Essays on Anita Hill, Clarence Thomas, and the Construction of Social Reality* (New York: Pantheon Books, 1992), which includes Wahneema Lubiano's "Black Ladies, Welfare Queens, and State Minstrels: Ideological War by Narrative Means," 323–63.
5   See Kimberlé Crenshaw's "Demarginalizing the Intersection of Race and Sex: A Black Feminist Critique of Antidiscrimination Doctrine, Feminist Theory, and Antiracist Politics," in *Feminism and Politics*, ed. A. Phillips (New York: Oxford University Press, 1998), 314–43, for an analysis of the ways that feminist, antiracist, and legal discourses obscure the experiences of

    African American women. See also Adrien Wing's anthology, *Critical Race Feminism: A Reader*, 2nd ed. (New York: New York University Press, 2003).

6   There are numerous stereotypes that have been applied to black women; these include but are not limited to mammy, sapphire, jezebel, the matriarch, the superwoman. See Leith Mullings' "Image, Ideology, and Women of Color," in Maxine Baca Zinn and Bonnie Thornton Dill's *Women of Color in U.S. Society* (Philadelphia: Temple University Press, 1994), 265–90, and Patricia Morton, *Disfigured Images: The Historical Assault on Afro-American Women* (Westport, Conn.: Greenwood Press, 1991), as well as a discussion of current incarnations of these stereotypes in Patricia Hill Collins' *Black Sexual Politics: African Americans, Gender and the New Racism* (New York: Routledge, 2004).

7   Iconic civil rights leaders Martin Luther King Jr. and Malcolm X have long been used to represent the tension between proponents of nonviolence and more radical notions of activism that promoted armed self-defense. See James H. Cone, *Martin & Malcolm & America: A Dream or a Nightmare* (Maryknoll, N.Y.: Orbis, 1991) and Britta Waldschmidt-Nelson, *Dreams and Nightmares: Martin Luther King Jr., Malcolm X, and the Struggle for Black Equality in America* (Gainesville: University Press of Florida, 2012).

8   In chapter 6 I discuss the controversy surrounding Jodi Kantor's book *The Obamas* (New York: Penguin, 2012) as an example of the persistence of the stereotype of the angry black woman and its use to dismiss strong, educated, and vocal African American women.

9   Leith Mullings' "Image, Ideology, and Women of Color" discusses the stereotypes of jezebel, mammy, matriarchs, and sapphire. See also Wahneema Lubiano's article "Black Ladies, Welfare Queens, and State Minstrels" and Patricia Hill Collins' discussion of the controlling images faced by African American women in *Black Feminist Thought: Knowledge, Consciousness, and the Politics of Empowerment* (Boston: Unwin Hyman, 1990).

10   See Nell Irvin Painter's "Representing Truth: Sojourner Truth's Knowing and Becoming Known," *Journal of American History* 81, no. 2 (1994): 461–92, and Paula Giddings' *When and Where I Enter: The Impact of Black Women on Race and Sex in America* (1984; repr., New York: HarperCollins, 1996) and *Ida: A Sword among Lions: Ida B. Wells and the Campaign against Lynching* (New York: HarperCollins, 2008) for historical accounts of the lives and work of Ida B. Wells and Sojourner Truth.

11   *The Narrative of Sojourner Truth* (1850; repr., Mineola, N.Y.: Dover, 1997) recounts the remarkable life and work of a woman who not only fought for her own freedom but also worked tirelessly for the freedom of others.

12   Wells' vocal challenge to "lynch law in America" made her the target of frequent death threats. Wells provided a scathing indictment of the failure of the American system of justice to protect black citizens from the horrific practice of lynching. See Gail Bederman's "'Civilization,' the Decline of Middle-Class Manliness, and Ida B. Wells' Antilynching Campaign (1892–94)," *Radical History Review* 52 (1992): 5–30.

13   For a comprehensive analysis of Sojourner Truth's life, image, and legacy,

see Nell Irvin Painter's *Sojourner Truth: A Life, a Symbol* (New York: Norton, 1997). See also Deborah Gray White's *Ar'n't I a Woman? Female Slaves in the Plantation South* (New York: Norton, 1999). The life and work of Ida B. Wells is thoroughly documented in Paula Giddings' *Ida: A Sword among Lions.*

14   For a comprehensive study of the racist beliefs about and depictions of blacks that pervaded society during the period, see Winthrop D. Jordan's *White over Black: American Attitudes toward the Negro, 1550-1812*, 2nd ed. (Chapel Hill: University of North Carolina Press, 2012). See also Deborah Gray White's *Ar'n't I a Woman?* and *A Shining Thread of Hope: The History of Black Women in America* by Darlene Clark Hine and Kathleen Thompson (New York: Broadway Books, 1998).

15   See Barbara Welter's "The Cult of True Womanhood: 1820-1860," *American Quarterly* 18, no. 2 (1966): 151-74. See also Darlene Clark Hine, "Rape and the Inner Lives of Black Women in the Middle West: Preliminary Thoughts on the Culture of Dissemblance," *Signs* 14 (1988): 912-20, for a discussion of the ways black women managed the negative stereotypes (used to justify the sexual abuse of women) that cast them as sexually depraved and immoral.

16   See Nell Irvin Painter's analysis and discussion of the way that Sojourner Truth fashioned herself in photographs and sold her image in "Representing Truth," 483-86.

17   See Darlene Clark Hine's "Rape and the Inner Lives of Black Women," 912-20.

18   See Nell Irvin Painter's "Representing Truth," 483-86.

19   See Melissa V. Harris-Perry's discussion of how the construction of the strong black woman functions as a "racial and citizenship imperative for black women" in *Sister Citizen: Shame, Stereotypes, and Black Women in America* (New Haven: Yale University Press, 2011), 21. See also Sheri Parks' *Fierce Angels: The Strong Black Woman in American Life and Culture* (New York: One World, 2010), in which she argues that all black women are expected to be strong and selfless, sometimes to their own detriment. She connects this expectation not only to the stereotypical image of mammy, but also to the African American community, in which they are expected to be supportive and work behind the scenes. She also emphasizes the serious emotional and physical toll that living up to these expectations takes on black women.

20   See *Disfigured Images* by Patricia Morton.

CHAPTER 2

1   See Melissa V. Harris-Perry's *Sister Citizen* and Sheri Parks' *Fierce Angels.*

2   During the sixties and seventies the Afro was worn as a part of the rejection of Eurocentric standards of beauty and the affirmation of Afrocentric beauty, which included the wearing of one's hair in its natural state. While there were women who wore their hair natural before this period, this was a pivotal moment for the style in terms of its association with a militant black power movement and its mass popularity among African

Americans. See Noliwe M. Rooks' *Hair Raising: Beauty, Culture, and African American Women* (New Brunswick, N.J.: Rutgers University Press, 1996) and Susannah Walker's *Style and Status: Selling Beauty to African American Women, 1920-1975* (Lexington: University Press of Kentucky, 2007) for detailed discussions of African American women and the politics of hair.

3   See *Women, Violence, and the Media: Readings in Feminist Criminology*, edited by Drew Humphries (Lebanon, N.H.: Northeastern University Press, 2009).

4   In *Living for the City: Migration, Education and the Rise of the Black Panther Party in Oakland, California* (Chapel Hill: University of North Carolina Press, 2010), Donna Jean Murch analyzes the historical emergence of the Black Panther Party as part of a larger process of the migration of African Americans from the South in search of educational and other opportunities in California. See also *Agents of Repression: The FBI's Secret Wars Against the Black Panther Party and the American Indian Movement*, 2nd ed. (Cambridge, Mass.: South End, 2001) by Ward Churchill and Jim Vander Wall for a discussion of coordinated efforts to crush black radicalism in the United States.

5   Huey P. Newton was the leader of the Black Panther Party. For more information see *To Die for the People: The Writings of Huey P. Newton*, edited by Toni Morrison and Elaine Brown (San Francisco: City Lights Books, 2009), as well as Judson L. Jeffries' *Huey P. Newton: The Radical Theorist* (Jackson: University Press of Mississippi, 2002).

6   See Ruth Rosen's *The World Split Open: How the Modern Women's Movement Changed America*, 2nd ed. (New York: Penguin, 2000) for an overview of the development of radical feminist organizations, like the Redstockings, that challenged liberal feminist approaches deployed by Betty Friedan and Gloria Steinem in organizations like NOW.

7   See *All the Women Are White, All the Blacks Are Men, but Some of Us Are Brave: Black Women Studies*, edited by Gloria T. Hull, Patricia Bell Scott, and Barbara Smith (New York: Feminist Press, 1982) and, more recently, *Still Brave: The Evolution of Black Women's Studies*, edited by Stanlie Myrise James, Frances Smith Foster, and Beverly Guy-Sheftall (New York: Feminist Press, 2009).

8   According to Joy James, Davis became an iconic figure of black revolutionary struggle despite the fact that most of her activism took place while she was working in other organizations like the Student Nonviolent Coordinating Committee and the Communist Party USA. Joy James, *Shadowboxing: Representations of Black Feminist Politics* (New York: St. Martin's, 1999), 204-5. See also *Resisting State Violence: Radicalism, Gender, and Race in U.S. Culture* (Minneapolis: University of Minnesota Press, 1996), by James.

9   In her autobiography, published in 1974, Davis discusses how angry she was when she saw a photograph of the three chained black male prisoners who were charged with the murder of a white prison guard at Soledad Prison. This would be catalyst for her decision to become an active member of the free the Soledad Brothers movement in Los Angeles. Angela Davis, *Angela Davis: An Autobiography* (1974; repr., New York: International Publishers, 1988), 250. See also James, *Resisting State Violence* and George

Jackson's *Soledad Brother: The Prison Letters of George Jackson* (1970; repr., New York: Lawrence Hill Books, 1994).

10 "Chancellor in a Crossfire," *Time*, May 18, 1970, 83.

11 She was later acquitted of all charges and released. Her experience in prison solidified her commitment to challenging the U.S. penal system.

12 "The Path of Angela Davis," *Life*, September 11, 1970, 20D–27.

13 "Path of Angela Davis," 20D.

14 "Path of Angela Davis," 21.

15 "Path of Angela Davis," 21.

16 "Path of Angela Davis," 21.

17 "Path of Angela Davis," 23.

18 "Path of Angela Davis," 25.

19 "Angela Davis Case," *Newsweek*, October 26, 1970, 18–24.

20 In *The Negro Family: The Case for National Action* (Washington, D.C.: U.S. Department of Labor, Office of Policy Planning and Research, 1965), Daniel Patrick Moynihan argues that slavery created a pattern of matriarchal leadership in the black family that caused the failure of black men to take their roles as the head of the family, which contributed to the downfall of the black family and community.

21 See Patricia Hill Collins' *Black Sexual Politics* for a discussion of how controlling images of black womanhood and stereotyping are used to stigmatize and stereotype black women who are aggressive about asserting themselves and their rights.

22 "White-on-White Jury for Angela Too!" *The Black Panther*, November 20, 1971, 2.

23 "Come Home Angela," *The Black Panther*, September 2, 1972, 3.

24 Cordell S. Thompson, "Angela Davis Case Puts Justice on Trial," *Jet*, May 6, 1971, 44.

25 Thompson, "Angela Davis Case," 45.

26 Thompson, "Angela Davis Case," 45.

27 Thompson, "Angela Davis Case," 45.

28 The case of Assata Shakur is noteworthy. For Shakur's account of her imprisonment, escape, and exile to Cuba, see *Assata: An Autobiography* (1987; repr., Chicago: Lawrence Hill Books, 2001).

29 Thompson, "Angela Davis Case," 48.

30 Thompson, "Angela Davis Case," 49.

31 Robert DeLeon, "A Revealing Report on Angela Davis' Fight for Freedom," *Jet*, November 18, 1971, 12–17.

32 DeLeon, "Revealing Report," 12.

33 DeLeon, "Revealing Report," 12.

34 DeLeon, "Revealing Report," 17.

35 Michele Wallace rebels against a narrative that features "Angela Davis, a brilliant, middle-class black woman, with a European education, a Ph.D. in philosophy, and a university appointment, was willing to die for a poor, uneducated black male inmate. It was straight out of Hollywood—Ingrid Bergman and Humphrey Bogart. For all her achievements, she was seen

134

as the epitome of the selfless, sacrificing 'good woman'—the only kind of woman the Movement would accept. She did it for her man, they said. A woman in a woman's place." Wallace, *Black Macho and the Myth of Super-woman* (1978; repr., London: Verso, 1999), 165–66.

36   Robert DeLeon, "A Look at Angela Davis from Another Angle: Her Jail Cell," *Jet*, February 24, 1972, 8.

37   DeLeon, "A Look at Angela Davis," 8.

38   DeLeon, "A Look at Angela Davis," 8.

39   DeLeon, "A Look at Angela Davis," 13.

40   DeLeon, "A Look at Angela Davis," 9.

41   Perhaps she felt the pressure to be strong and selfless discussed in Parks' *Fierce Angels*.

42   Robert DeLeon, "Angela Davis Works to Bring Change in Prison System," *Jet*, May 16, 1974, 12.

43   DeLeon, "Angela Davis Works," 18.

44   See Erika Doss' "Revolutionary Art Is a Tool for Liberation: Emory Douglas and Protest Aesthetics at *The Black Panther*," *New Political Science* 21, no. 2 (1999): 245–59.

45   Kathleen Neal Cleaver, "Women, Power and Revolution," *New Political Science* 21, no. 2 (1999): 233.

46   Tracye Matthews, "'No One Ever Asks, What a Man's Place in the Revolution Is': Gender and the Politics of the Black Panther Party 1966–1971," in *The Black Panther Party Reconsidered*, ed. Charles E. Jones (Baltimore: Black Classic Press, 1998), 267–304.

47   See *Dangerous Curves: Action Heroines, Gender, Fetishism, and Popular Culture* (Jackson: University Press of Mississippi, 2011), by Jeffrey A. Brown for discussion of the ways that gun-toting women are depicted in popular culture.

48   James, *Shadowboxing*, 103–4.

49   "The Revolutionary Spirit of Antonio Maceo Lives on Today . . .," *The Black Panther*, August 16, 1969, 3.

50   See Beverly Walker's discussion in "Michelangelo and the Leviathan: The Making of *Zabriskie Point*," *Film Comment*, September–October 1992, 36.

51   Christopher Porterfield, "Recycling Job," *Time*, April 18, 1977, 82.

52   Slang for an erection.

53   John Cocchi, "Edward and Mildred Lewis on Tour Promoting 'Brothers,' WB Release," *Box Office*, April 11, 1977, 5.

54   Cocchi, "Edward and Mildred Lewis," 5.

CHAPTER 3

1   Randall Clark identifies these conventions of blaxploitation film in his book about the broader genre of exploitation films, *At a Theater or Drive-In Near You: The History, Culture and Politics of the American Exploitation Film* (New York: Garland, 1995), 5, 152. See also Mikel J. Koven's *The Pocket Essential Blaxploitation Films* (Harpenden, UK: Pocket Essentials, 2001) and Ed Guerrero's *Framing Blackness: The African American Image in Film* (Philadelphia: Temple University Press, 1993).

2 Donald Bogle makes this argument in *Toms, Coons, Mulattoes, Mammies, &*
   Bucks: An Interpretive History of Blacks in American Films, 3rd ed. (New York:
   Continuum, 1996), 236. See also Bogle's *Blacks in American Films and Tele-*
   vision: An Illustrated Encyclopedia (New York: Simon & Schuster, 1988) for
   more information about the depiction of African Americans in film.

3 Melvin Van Peeble's *Sweetback* was followed by a series of Hollywood films
   such as *Shaft* (Gordon Parks Jr., 1971), *Superfly* (Gordon Parks Jr., 1972), and
   Bucktown (Arthur Marks, 1973), which were designed to exploit the black
   audiences' enthusiastic response to the new genre of black-themed action
   films (Bogle, *Toms*, 238).

4 In fact black civil rights organizations like the National Association for the
   Advancement of Colored People (NAACP) organized campaigns against
   the genre in an attempt to convince Hollywood to provide more positive
   representations of African Americas.

5 See Stephane Dunn's *"Baad Bitches" & Sassy Supermamas: Black Power Action*
   Films (Urbana: University of Illinois Press, 2008) and Yvonne D. Sims'
   Women of Blaxploitation: How the Black Action Film Heroine Changed American
   Popular Culture (Jefferson, N.C.: McFarland, 2006).

6 Yvonne Tasker's *Spectacular Bodies: Gender, Genre and the Action Cinema*
   (London: Routledge, 1993), 19, highlights the extent to which representations of active heroines compensate for their power by emphasizing traditional feminine sexuality and availability.

7 See Wallace's *Black Macho*, 138.

8 In "Visual Pleasure and Narrative Cinema," in *Feminism and Film Theory*, ed.
   Constance Penley (New York: Routledge, 1988), 62, Laura Mulvey argued
   that classic Hollywood cinema privileges a male gaze and projects its fantasy on the female figure.

9 In "Blaxploitation and the Misrepresentation of Liberation," *Race and*
   Class: A Journal for Black and Third World Liberation 40, no. 1 (1998): 5–6,
   Cedric Robinson reads blaxploitation as a misrepresentation of black liberation and argues that these films misappropriated the images of real
   revolutionary women, like Angela Davis. His reading of blaxploitation film
   is similar to that of other critics who have focused overwhelmingly on the
   ways that black nationalism has been commodified and "reinscribed and
   marketed with an atavistic narrative, a fantasy of Otherness that reduces
   protest to spectacle" (hooks, *Black Looks: Race and Representation* [Cam-
   bridge, Mass.: South End, 1992], 33).

10 See Ed Guerrero's *Framing Blackness*, 98.

11 Rather than viewing the cinematic apparatus as constructing and stabiliz-
   ing the viewer into an unchanging and predetermined relationship to the
   screen, feminist film theory has tried to account for the ways that female
   spectators negotiate the cinematic apparatus. Based on critiques of her
   essay "Visual Pleasure and Narrative Cinema," Laura Mulvey revised her
   analysis of female spectatorship to consider the possibility that female
   viewers can shift between passive identification and a more active
   identification, which she had previously defined as masculine. Mulvey,

"Afterthoughts on 'Visual Pleasure and Narrative Cinema' Inspired by *Dual in the Sun*," in Penley, *Feminism and Film Theory*, 69–79, 72.

12 *The L Word* was a groundbreaking and very popular series on Showtime that followed the lives of LA lesbians. Grier played Kit, the half sister of Bette, played by Jennifer Beals.

13 Recall that the wearing of one's hair in an Afro had come to represent an archetypal representation of black womanhood that was associated with black nationalism and revolutionary politics. See Althea Prince's *The Politics of Black Women's Hair* (London: Insomniac Press, 2009) and Ayana Byrd and Lori Tharps' *Hair Story: Untangling the Roots of Black Hair in America* (New York: St. Martin's, 2001).

14 This is an example of the complex ways that the juxtaposition of African American women and white women provides the potential for reading same-sex desire.

15 See Elaine Brown's *A Taste of Power: A Black Woman's Story* (New York: Pantheon Books, 1992) and Angela LeBlanc-Ernest's "'The Most Qualified Person to Handle the Job': Black Panther Party Women, 1966–1971," in Jones, *Black Panther Party Reconsidered*, 305–34.

16 *Race Traitor*, edited by Noel Ignatiev and John Garvey (New York: Routledge, 1996), contains essays that explore the construction of white identity and its relationship to racial politics and oppression.

17 See James' *Shadowboxing* and Wallace's *Black Macho*.

18 According to Sarah Projansky, "[Rape narratives] help organize, understand, and even arguably produce the social world; they help structure social understandings of complex phenomena such as gender, race, class, and nation. Additionally, they help inscribe a way of looking, the conditions of watching, and the attitudes and structures of feeling one might have about rape, women and people of color" (*Watching Rape: Film and Television in Postfeminist Culture* [New York: New York University Press, 2001], 7).

19 Mary Ann Doane's psychoanalytic analysis of *Imitation of Life* (Douglas Sirk, 1959) emphasizes the interconnection between "the hypersexualization of the black woman, her association with an unrestrained promiscuity which left the white woman free to occupy the pedestal of sexual purity." Doane, *Femme Fatales: Feminism, Film Theory, Psychoanalysis* (New York: Routledge, 1991), 243. While Doane's discussion is primarily focused on an analysis of the genre of the "woman's film," her point is significant to a textual analysis of the ways that representations of black women and white women in films featuring Grier work in the construction of the binary oppositions of white femininity and black femininity. Her analysis reinforces scholarship by African American feminists who critique the ideals of white femininity and beauty by which black women have been historically judged.

20 For example, in both *Cleopatra Jones* and *Foxy Brown*, each black female lead has a white female enemy. In *Cleopatra Jones* Shelly Winters plays a ruthless lesbian drug lord who wreaks havoc on an urban neighborhood, and in *Foxy Brown* there is a famous lesbian bar scene where Foxy saves her

friend from the advances of a white lesbian. See Kelly Hankin's *The Girls in the Back Room: Looking at the Lesbian Bar* (Minneapolis: University of Minnesota Press, 2002) for an analysis of how the lesbian bar scene functions in a variety of contexts.

21 Dunn, *"Baad Bitches"* and Tasker, *Spectacular Bodies*.

22 *Black Mama, White Mama* (Eddie Romero, 1972), one of the first films featuring Pam Grier, has a female prison guard who pursues inmates sexually. Grier's white female costar from *The Arena*, Margaret Markov, plays a white female revolutionary who ultimately submits to the guard's advances. Lee, the character played by Grier, resists the advance and is punished as a result. See Judith Mayne's *Framed: Lesbians, Feminists, and Media Culture* (Minneapolis: University of Minnesota Press, 2000), 138, for an analysis of how the racial plot and the lesbian plot rely on each other. In "Caged Heat: The (R)evolution of Women-in-Prison Films," in *Reel Knockouts: Violent Women in the Movies*, ed. Martha McCaughey and Neal King (Austin: University of Texas Press, 2001), 106. Suzanna Walters argues that "women-prison films elaborate fully the creation of the marginal subject."

23 See Lorde's discussion of lesbian baiting in *Sister Outsider: Essays and Speeches by Audre Lorde* (Berkeley, Calif.: Crossing Press, 1984) as well as Evelyn Hammonds' "Black (W)holes and the Geometry of Black Female Sexuality," in *African American Literary Theory: A Reader*, ed. W. Napier (New York: New York University Press, 2000), 482–97.

24 This visual representation reinforces and strengthens a "culture of dissemblance" that makes it acceptable for black lesbians to be considered traitors to the race (Hammonds, "Black (W)holes," 491).

25 "Pam Grier Finds Fame in Black Movie Films," *Jet*, August 9, 1973, 59.

26 "Pam Grier Finds Fame," 60.

27 "Pam Grier Finds Fame," 60.

28 "Pam Grier Finds Fame," 61.

29 See Nancy Friday's *My Secret Garden: Women's Sexual Fantasies* (1973; repr., New York: Pocket Books, 2008).

30 "Pam Grier Finds Fame," 61.

31 Two years later, in August 1975, Grier graced the cover of the feminist magazine *Ms*. In Jamaica Kincaid's feature article on Grier, she discusses how despite the stereotypes, Grier's films provided an image of a black woman who triumphs. She also discusses Grier's frustration with those in Hollywood who were interested only in reproducing the same old narratives of the angry, vengeful black woman (52–53).

32 See Pam Grier's memoir, *Foxy: My Life in Three Acts* (New York: Springboard Press, 2010), in which she discusses her life and career and the many challenges of being a black female actress in Hollywood.

33 Numerous scholars, such as Judith Mayne, Patricia White, and Jacqueline Bobo, have tried to make sense of female spectatorship in light of the overwhelming evidence that classic Hollywood cinema addresses the male spectator.

34 In *Black Women as Cultural Readers* (New York: Columbia University Press,

138

1995), Jacqueline Bobo uses this term to describe groups of spectators, specifically black female spectators and the way that they interpret popular culture (22).

35 Donald Bogle argues that most black women found it difficult to relate to the black heroines in blaxploitation films. Bogle's assumption that black women could not relate to the characters in Grier's films assumes that black female spectators could not possibly find other points of pleasure beyond identification with the heroine. It also ignores the actual evidence that there were black women who were in some ways drawn to these images. Bogle, *Blacks in American Films*, 251.

36 See Dunn's *"Baad Bitches."*

37 Cultural critic Lisa Jones argues that despite the negativity of these depictions of black womanhood, Cleopatra Jones and Foxy Brown "raised Hollywood's threshold of black female visibility. Whatever you say about Cleo and Foxy, they are not shuffling mammies, teary-eyed mulattoes, or boozy blues singers. They talk back." Lisa Jones, *Bulletproof Diva: Tales of Race, Sex, and Hair* (New York: Anchor Books/Doubleday, 1994), 85.

38 hooks, *Black Looks*, 199.

39 Such a reading would challenge Jennifer DeVere Brody's suggestion that Pam Grier's portrayal of *Foxy Brown* is less conducive to a queer reading than Tamara Dobson's portrayal of *Cleopatra Jones*. Jennifer DeVere Brody, "The Return of Cleopatra Jones," *Signs: Journal of Women in Culture and Society* 25, no. 1 (1999): 93–96. Patricia White's analysis of lesbian spectatorship in her book *Uninvited: Classical Hollywood Cinema and Lesbian Representability* (Bloomington: Indiana University Press, 1999) is an important resource for understanding how lesbian spectators subvert classic heterosexual narratives through a complex process of finding potential points of same-sex desire and lesbian subjectivity in mainstream films that privilege heterosexual spectators.

40 Guerrero, *Framing Blackness*, 99.

41 Hankin, *Girls in the Back Room*, argues that Inyang's film explores her frustrated identification with and desire for Grier, as well as her examination of the sexism within blaxploitation films (83). In addition, she sees Inyang's "celluloid" plastic surgery of *Foxy Brown* into the remake *Badass Supermama* as "an act of unwavering cinephilia" (113) that provides another way to understand Pam Grier's star image as transcending the blaxploitation box to which she has largely been relegated.

42 Sharon Willis, *High Contrast: Race and Gender in Contemporary Hollywood Film* (Durham, N.C.: Duke University Press, 1997), 197.

43 Gerald Perry, *Quentin Tarantino: Interviews* (Jackson: University Press of Mississippi, 1998), 199.

44 *Jackie Brown: Collector's Edition*, 2002.

45 Quentin Tarantino, *Jackie Brown: A Quentin Tarantino Screenplay* (New York: Miramax Books, 1997), 230.

1   Bebe Moore Campbell, "What Happened to the Afro?: Changing Hairstyles Reflect New Roles and New Definitions," *Ebony*, June 1982, 79–85. Campbell explores the social and political factors that contributed to the rise of the Afro hairstyle's popularity as well as the growing conservatism in the United States and middle-class blacks that ultimately led to a decline in the style's popularity.

2   Campbell, "What Happened to the Afro?"

3   In addition to Alice Walker and Audre Lorde, numerous African American women produced texts that challenged existing stereotypes about black women. I focus on Lorde and Walker because of the way that they use the image of the Amazon in their texts. In addition, I argue that Walker's *The Color Purple* (Orlando, Fla.: Harcourt, 1982), and its filmic adaptation, was an important influence on young black women who were coming of age in the 1980s, who later used revolutionary iconography in their artistic productions.

4   See Jacqueline Bobo's *Black Women as Cultural Readers* for a study of black female spectatorship and the reception of Walker's film.

5   The film was controversial for several reasons. First, Steven Spielberg, a white man, directed the film. Second, Walker decided to use a screenplay written by Menno Meyjes instead of her own version of the screenplay. There was also controversy about the on-screen kiss between Margaret Avery and Whoopi Goldberg.

6   Ishmael Reed was very critical of Alice Walker's work and heavily critiqued what he characterized as the airing of dirty laundry by black women writers. See his book of essays, *Airing Dirty Laundry* (New York: Perseus, 1995). See Trudier Harris' critique of the novel and its elevation to the canon of black literature in "On *The Color Purple*, Stereotypes, and Silence," *Black American Literature Forum* 18 (1984): 155–61.

7   Writers such as Michele Wallace, Ntozake Shangé, and other African American women were attacked by black male scholars, such as Robert Staples. Alice Walker wrote a memo to the editors of *The Black Scholar*, but they refused to publish her response. Walker published the memo in *In Search of Our Mothers' Gardens: Womanist Prose* (New York: Harcourt Brace Jovanovich, 1984).

8   Walker has a lengthy definition of womanism that is included in her book of essays, *In Search of Our Mothers' Gardens*.

9   See Lorde's "The Uses of Anger: Women Responding to Racism," in her book of essays, *Sister Outsider*, 124-33.

10 See Lorde's "Age, Race, Class, and Sex: Women Redefining Difference," in *Sister Outsider*, 114-23.

11 In her essay "The Transformation of Silence into Language and Action," Lorde states, "[I]n the cause of silence, each of us draws the face of her own fear—fear of contempt, of censure, or some judgment, or recognition, of challenge, of annihilation. But most of all, I think we fear the visibility without which we cannot truly live. . . . And the visibility which makes us

most vulnerable is that which is also our greatest strength" (Lorde, *Sister Outsider*, 41-43).

12 In "Towards a Black Feminist Criticism," in Hull, Scott, and Smith, *All the Women Are White*, 159, Barbara Smith questions whether traditional literary theory can be used to understand the work of black women, such as Toni Morrison and Alice Walker. She also calls for a black feminist criticism that addresses not only sexism but also the heterosexism and homophobia manifested in the criticism of black feminist literature. She explores how through reading against the grain or between the lines one can find multiple meanings within a text. For example, her controversial reading of Morrison's *Sula* as a lesbian text, which was denied by Morrison, underscores how the emphasis placed on intimacy between women is privileged over heterosexual relationships in the novel. Her framework emphasizes the complexities of meaning production and a close consideration of "the distinctive signifying properties" of the text and "specific emotional and experiential histories" of readers. Smith, "Towards a Black Feminist Criticism," 180. See also Barbara Christian's *Black Women Novelists: The Development of a Tradition, 1892-1976* (Westport, Conn.: Greenwood Press, 1980) for an extensive discussion of the novels of Alice Walker.

13 See Wallace's *Black Macho*.

14 See Alan Nadel's "Reading the Body: *Meridian* and the Archeology of Self" (155-67) and Wendy Wall's "Lettered Bodies and the Corporeal Texts" (261-74), in *Alice Walker: Critical Perspectives Past and Present*, ed. Henry Louis Gates, Jr. and K. A. Appiah (New York: Amistad Press, 1993).

15 Audre Lorde, *Zami: A New Spelling of My Name* (Berkeley, Calif.: Crossing Press, 1982), 3.

16 bell hooks argues that Walker's *The Color Purple* is a revolutionary text because it "has as its central goal the education for critical consciousness, creating awareness of the forces that oppress and recognition of the way those forces might be transformed." hooks, "Reading and Resistance: *The Color Purple*," in Gates and Appiah, *Alice Walker: Critical Perspectives*, 292.

17 Walker, *The Color Purple*, 21.

18 See Cynthia Ellers, *Gentlemen and Amazons: The Myth of Matriarchal Prehistory, 1861-1900* (Berkeley: University of California Press, 2011); and Stanley B. Alpern, *Amazons of Black Sparta: The Women Warriors of Dahomey* (1998; repr., London: C. Hurst, 2011).

19 Walker, *The Color Purple*, 30.

20 Walker, *The Color Purple*, 30.

21 Walker, *The Color Purple*, 30.

22 Walker, *The Color Purple*, 36.

23 Walker, *The Color Purple*, 37.

24 Walker, *The Color Purple*, 40.

25 Walker, *The Color Purple*, 67.

26 See Thomas F. Marvin's analysis of Walker's use of the figure of the blues singer in "'Preachin' the Blues': Bessie Smith's Secular Religion and Alice Walker's *The Color Purple*," *African American Review* 28 (1994): 411-21.

27 Walker, *The Color Purple*, 6.

28 Walker, *The Color Purple*, 7.

29 In "Race, Gender and Nation in *The Color Purple*," Lauren Berlant argues that even at a young age Celie learns from Shug's picture "the connection between male sexual desire and the desire to degrade women" in Gates and Appiah, *Alice Walker*, 214.

30 Walker, *The Color Purple*, 24–25.

31 Walker, *The Color Purple*, 24–25.

32 Walker, *The Color Purple*, 24–25.

33 Walker, *The Color Purple*, 49.

34 Walker, *The Color Purple*, 51.

35 Walker, *The Color Purple*, 51.

36 Walker, *The Color Purple*, 51.

37 Walker, *The Color Purple*, 53.

38 Walker, *The Color Purple*, 53.

39 Walker, *The Color Purple*, 72.

40 Walker, *The Color Purple*, 73.

41 Walker, *The Color Purple*, 73.

42 Walker, *The Color Purple*, 77.

43 Walker, *The Color Purple*, 77.

44 Walker, *The Color Purple*, 78.

45 Walker, *The Color Purple*, 77–78.

46 Walker, *The Color Purple*, 113–14.

47 Quincy Jones produced *The Color Purple*. Oprah Winfrey would go on to produce works by Toni Morrison, Zora Neal Hurston, and Gloria Naylor. She also has been criticized for altering aspects of these classic works.

48 In the special features portion of the 2003 DVD release of film, Walker explains that she was not satisfied with her initial attempt at writing the screenplay and decided not to use it. Instead, she decided to go with a screenplay written by Menno Meyjes. However, Walker was on the set daily and had an important impact on the film.

49 In the novel, when Mister threatens to slap Celie at the dinner table, she stabs the knife into his hand (Walker, *The Color Purple*, 200).

50 The Kitchen Table Women of Color Press was founded by Barbara Smith, Audre Lorde, Cherríe Moraga, and other women of color scholars who were writing in the eighties. See Barbara Smith's "A Press of Our Own: Kitchen Table: Women of Color Press," which was published in *Frontiers* in 1989 (vol. 10, no. 3, pp. 11–13). This press played an important role in the distribution of the scholarly work of women of color.

51 Lorde, *Sister Outsider*, 53.

52 In *Blues Legacies and Black Feminism* (1998; repr., New York: Vintage, 1999), Angela Davis asks, "What can we learn from women like Gertrude 'Ma' Rainey, Bessie Smith, and Billie Holiday that we may not be able to learn from Ida B. Wells, Anna Julia Cooper, and Mary Church Terrell? If we were beginning to appreciate the blasphemies of fictionalized blues women—especially their outrageous politics of sexuality—and the knowledge that

142 might be gleaned from their lives about the possibilities of transforming gender relations within black communities, perhaps we also could benefit from a look at the artistic contributions of the original blues women" (xiv).

53 See Jacqueline Bobo's *Black Women as Cultural Readers* for a discussion of the responses of black female spectators to *The Color Purple*.

54 Alice Walker, "'I Am a Renegade, an Outlaw, a Pagan' —Author, Poet, and Activist Alice Walker in Her Own Words," interview by Amy Goodman, *DemocracyNow.org*, February 13, 2006, http://www.democracynow.org/2006/2/13/i_am_a_renegade_an_outlaw.

55 Walker, "'I Am a Renegade.'"

56 Lorde, *Zami*, 176.

57 Lorde, *Zami*, 15.

58 Lorde, *Zami*, 15.

59 Lorde, *Zami*, 104 (emphasis in original).

60 Lorde, *Zami*, 169.

61 Lorde, *The Cancer Journals* (San Francisco: Aunt Lute Books, 1980), 28.

62 Lorde, *Zami*, 250.

63 Lorde, *Zami*, 255–56 (emphasis in original).

CHAPTER 5

1 See Tricia Rose's *Black Noise: Rap Music and Black Culture in Contemporary America* (Hanover, N.H.: University Press of New England, 1994), Gwendolyn D. Pough's *Check It while I Wreck It: Black Womanhood, Hip Hop Culture, and the Public Sphere* (Boston: Northeastern University Press, 2004), Imani Perry's *Prophets of the Hood: Politics and Poetics in Hip Hop* (Durham, N.C.: Duke University Press, 2004), and Mark Anthony Neal's *Songs in the Key of Black Life: A Rhythm and Blues Nation* (New York: Routledge, 2003).

2 In *From Black Power to Hip Hop: Racism, Nationalism, and Feminism* (Philadelphia: Temple University Press, 2006), Patricia Hill Collins discusses how young women in the hip-hop generation "who do manage to find feminism increasingly carve out a space that simultaneously accepts and rejects the tenets of feminism and nationalism. Specifically, they may be transforming the core feminist ideology that the personal is political in response to the challenges that confront them" (162).

3 Susan Kaplow, "Behind the Scenes with Erykah Badu," *Seventeen*, June 1997, 108.

4 Despite the consumerist culture in which these artists exist, scholars such as Tricia Rose contend that "commodified cultural production is a *deeply but crucial* terrain for developing politically progressive expression at this historical moment" (emphasis in original). Rose, "Cultural Survivalisms and Marketplace Subversions: Black Popular Culture and Politics into the Twenty-First Century," in *Language, Rhythm, and Sound: Black Popular Cultures into the Twenty-First Century*, ed. Joseph Adjaye and Adrianne R. Andrews (Pittsburgh: University of Pittsburgh Press, 1997), 263. This is true for black women who historically have been marginalized and objectified in the hip-hop industry. There are strong messages within this

music about the place of black women, in both their communities and the world.

5   During the sixties and seventies, many African Americans took on African names or constructed what would later become African American names as a direct form of resistance and affirmation of their African heritage. One major example is the nation of Islam's use of "X" as a last name because it specifically rejected "slave names" given to enslaved Africans. See Joel McIver's discussion of Badu's decision to change her name in *Erykah Badu: The First Lady of Neo-Soul* (London: Sanctuary, 2002), 33.

6   McIver, *Erykah Badu*, 33.

7   McIver, *Erykah Badu*, 32.

8   McIver, *Erykah Badu*, 43.

9   Othermothers are other women, such as aunts, grandmothers, and other black women in the community, who support biological mothers or blood-mothers. For a broader discussion of this practice in the African American community, see Patricia Hill Collins, *Black Feminist Thought*, 178–82.

10   McLean Greaves, "Me'shell Ndegéocello: A Sista from Another Planet," *Essence*, September 1996, 95–96.

11   Some might question whether this aspect of the new wave in young black female artists is a reflection of young black women's consciousness and direct interest in embracing the African past or aesthetic or whether it is driven by a consumer culture that has commodified the ethnic other and Afrocentricity.

12   McIver, *Erykah Badu*, 17.

13   Also spelled *dreadlocks*, this hairstyle is part of the Rastafarian religion. However, this hairstyle has recently gained popularity among African Americans who do not identify as Rastafarian.

14   *Plantation Lullabies* (1993).

15   Despite her openness about her bisexuality, some gays and lesbians complained that she avoided it her music. See Wendy Jill York's article, "Luck Star," which was featured in *The Advocate* on October 19, 1993.

16   *Baduizm* (1997).

17   *Baduizm* (1997).

18   See Paula Giddings' *When and Where I Enter*.

19   The Sugar Water Festival, LLC, owned by Erykah Badu, Queen Latifah, and Jill Scott, was founded in 2005 to showcase the music of black women through a multicity tour.

20   *Baduizm* (1997).

21   See Angela Y. Davis' *Blues Legacies and Black Feminism*.

22   Aretha Franklin's classic single "Respect" is another anthem that has inspired women to resist abuse at the hands of their abusive partners.

23   *Plantation Lullabies* (1993).

24   Sonia Murray, "Song for a Friend," *Atlanta Journal-Constitution*, August 12, 1993, n.p.

25   *Baduizm* (1997).

26   *Baduizm* (1997).

144 27 *Baduizm* (1997).

28 In "Badu's Groove," featured in the August 1997 issue of *Essence*, Michael Gonzales argues that Badu's choices in this video "conjures up hoodoo folklore, Black Nationalist chic and hip-hop bohemianism [and challenges] the cult of Black pop video hoochies" (92).

29 Original art by EMEK featured on Erykah Badu's website can be found at http://emek.net/posters/b/badu_covers_2008.html.

30 During the seventies many black nationalist organizations promoted the idea that one major contribution of African American women is the bearing and raising of future black revolutionaries.

31 Deborah Gregory, "Erykah Badu: Feel Her Flow," *Essence*, April 1997, 66.

32 John Morthland, "The Voice of Amerykah," *Texas Monthly*, May 1997, 58.

33 The video for "Bag Lady" draws on imagery from the feminist poet, novelist, and playwright Ntozake Shange and her critically acclaimed play, *For Colored Girls Who Have Considered Suicide/When the Rainbow Is Enuf.*

34 In his *Hip Hoptionary: A Dictionary of Hip Hop Terminology*, Alonzo Westbrook defines "freak" as "a sexually charged or sexually aggressive person" (50). However, he does not note that the term is used almost exclusively to describe women.

35 Imani Perry, *Prophets of the Hood*, argues that "the visual landscape of women hip hop artists represents the contested terrain of the black female body in the music, and made it clear how fraught with sexism and objectification hip hop is, even for the feminists or self-articulating women in the culture" (156). She also notes that many of the women who were challenging the previous mainstream conceptions of female beauty promoted by mainstream culture, such as Lauryn Hill, Queen Latifah, and Erykah Badu, would find it necessary to draw on mainstream expressions of female beautification and sexuality that involved sexual objectification (156).

36 Vonnie Woods, honeysoul.com, March 2007.

37 Interview for *Pop Matters*, 2009.

38 Interview for *Pop Matters*, 2009.

39 See Parks, *Fierce Angels.*

40 See chapter 1 of Neal's *Songs in the Key of Black Life* for an analysis of Ndegéocello's *Cookie: The Anthropological Mixtape.*

41 *Cookie: The Anthropological Mixtape* (2002).

42 Imani Perry, *Prophets of the Hood*, 156, discusses the ways that black female rappers and performers use a masculinist performance as a way to navigate the male-dominated world of hip-hop. See also Joan Morgan's *When Chickenheads Come Home to Roost: My Life as a Hip-Hop Feminist* (New York: Simon & Schuster, 1999) for a personal account of how women in the nineties negotiated their love of hip-hop and rap while simultaneously critiquing the misogyny that became a central part of the genre.

43 Ndegéocello uses this term in her song "Hot Night," featured on her album *Cookie: The Anthropological Mixtape* (2002).

44 Judith Halberstam, *Female Masculinity* (Durham, N.C.: Duke University Press, 1998), 177.

45 Kathy Dobie, "The Aggressives," *Vibe*, January 2003, 107.
46 In "'Ghetto Heaven': *Set It Off* and the Valorization of Black Lesbian Butch-Femme Sociality," *The Black Scholar* 33, no. 1 (2003), Kara Keeling argues that the continued use of butch-femme identity is a recognizable practice among black lesbians that serves several functions. "First, butch-femme still meets certain needs, whether erotic, economic, and/or something else, for certain living beings. As an element of black lesbian common sense, butch-femme contains nodes of consent to dominant hegemonies and it often enforces a rather rigid behavioral and aesthetic code that may have out-lived its usefulness for some. At the same time, however, butch-femme also is a malleable and dynamic form of sociality that still functions as a vehicle for the survival of forms of 'black lesbian' community, as a source of erotic tension and fulfillment, and as a set of personal gender choices and expressions. Because butch-femme is connected to issues of survival, it has become a mechanism for recognizing 'black lesbians' and for organizing 'black lesbian' sociality" (42).
47 The foundation of this resistance is what bell hooks calls "loving blackness as political resistance" (hooks, *Black Looks*, 10).
48 Lynn Darling, "Speaking the Unspoken," *Harper's Bazaar*, March 1994, 178.
49 Darling, "Speaking the Unspoken," 178.
50 Darling, "Speaking the Unspoken," 178.
51 *Plantation Lullabies* (1993).

CHAPTER 6

1 Susan Saulny, "Michelle Obama Thrives in Campaign Trenches," *New York Times*, February 14, 2008, http://www.nytimes.com/2008/02/14/us/politics/14michelle.html?pagewanted=print.
2 Diane Salvatore, "The Presidential Race Part I: The Obamas," *Ladies' Home Journal*, September 2008, 124.
3 Salvatore, "Presidential Race," 124.
4 CSPAN aired this video on February 18, 2008.
5 See Gregory S. Parks and Quinetta M. Roberson's "Michelle Obama: 'The Darker Side' of Presidential Spousal Involvement and Activism" (Cornell Law Faculty Working Papers, paper 39, 2008), http://scholarship.law.cornell.edu/clsops_papers/39; and "Hillary Clinton, Sarah Palin, and Michelle Obama: Performing Gender, Race, and Class on the Campaign Trail" by Ann C. McGinley (Scholarly Works, paper 171, 2009), http://scholars.law.unlv.edu/facpub/171.
6 "Michelle Obama and the Media," *Fox News Watch*, June 14, 2008.
7 The panel included Jane Hall of American University; syndicated columnist Cal Thomas; Jim Pinkerton, contributing editor and writer for the *American Conservative*; and Jonathan Martin, senior political writer for *Politico*.
8 "Michelle Obama and the Media," *Fox New Watch*, June 14, 2008.
9 See Patricia Hill Collins' *Black Sexual Politics* for a discussion of the ways that the controlling stereotypical image of "the black bitch" is deployed

to censure poor and working-class women who refuse to passively accept inequality. The label is used against educated African American women as well.

10 See *Stories of Oprah: The Oprahfication of American Culture* (Jackson: University Press of Mississippi, 2010) by Trystan Cotten and Kimberly Springer and *The Oprah Phenomenon* (Lexington: University Press of Kentucky, 2007) by Jennifer Harris and Elwood Watson for analyses of the importance of Oprah's public persona in popular culture.

11 The primary charge leveled against Angela Davis was that she was the mastermind of the escape plot of the Soledad Brothers. Assata Shakur is another example of a black woman who was active in the black nationalist movement of the seventies who was accused of being the mastermind behind the action of black men.

12 Jon Cohen and Michael D. Shear, "Poll Shows More Americans Think Obama Is a Muslim," *Washington Post*, August 19, 2010, http://www.washingtonpost.com/wp-dyn/content/article/2010/08/18/AR2010081806913_pf.html.

13 See Noliwe Rooks' *Hair Raising* and Ayana Byrd and Lori Tharps' *Hair Story*.

14 Robin Givhan, "Why a Hairstyle Made Headlines," *Washington Post*, April 7, 2006, http://www.washingtonpost.com/wp-dyn/content/article/2006/04/06/AR2006040602341_pf.html.

15 Givhan, "Why a Hairstyle Made Headlines."

16 Amy Argetsinger and Roxanne Roberts, "The Fist Couple: Giving a Big Bump to Authenticity," *Washington Post*, June 5, 2008, http://www.washingtonpost.com/wp-dyn/content/article/2008/06/04/AR2008060404521_pf.html.

17 Argetsinger and Roberts, "The Fist Couple."

18 John Cloud, "Fist Bump," number 4 in "The Top 10 Everything of 2008: The Top 10 Buzzwords," *Time*, November 3, 2008, http://www.time.com/time/specials/packages/article/0,28804,1855948_1864100_1864104,00.html.

19 The fist bump is also called giving "dap," a common greeting usually between black men to greet each other. In many cases it is used as a celebratory gesture, to show agreement, affirmation, or a job well done. See Westbrook, *Hip Hoptionary*.

20 Argetsinger and Roberts, "Fist Couple."

21 Sandra Sobieraj Westfall, "Michelle Obama: We're Home," *People* 71, no. 9, March 9, 2009, 114.

22 "'Welfare Queen' Becomes Issue in Reagan Campaign," *New York Times*, February 15, 1976, 51, http://select.nytimes.com/gst/abstract.html?res=FA0614FB395910728DDDAC0994DA405B868BF1D3&scp=2&sq=Welfare%20Queen%20and%20Reagan%20Campaign&st=cse.

23 See Susan Douglas and Meredith W. Michaels' *The Mommy Myth: The Idealization of Motherhood and How It Has Undermined All Women* (New York: Free Press, 2004).

24 In *Hip Hoptionary*, Alonzo Westbrook defines "baby momma" as "the mother of a man's child when the parents are not married" (6).

25 See Alex Koppelman's "Fox News Calls Michelle Obama 'Obama's Baby Mama,' The Sacred Community" *Salon.com*, June 11, 2008, http://www .salon.com/2008/06/12/fox_obama/.

26 Allison Samuels, "What Michelle Means to Us," *Newsweek*, December 1, 2008, 32.

27 Westfall, "Michelle Obama," 118.

28 Westfall, "Michelle Obama," 118.

29 Moynihan's report, *The Negro Family: The Case for National Action*, was criticized for the ways that it blames the emasculation of black men by black mothers as one of the causes of the cycle that keeps blacks in poverty. See Robert Staples, "The Myth of the Black Matriarchy," *The Black Scholar* 1 (1970): 9–16; and Katheryn Thomas Dietrick, "A Reexamination of the Myth of the Black Matriarchy," *Journal of Marriage and Family* 37 (1975): 367–74. See also Patricia Morton, *Disfigured Images*.

30 See Lisa M. Anderson's *Mammies No More: The Changing Image of Black Women on Stage and Screen* (Lanham, Md.: Rowman & Littlefield, 1997) and Beretta E. Smith Shomade's *Shaded Lives: African-American Women and Television* (New Brunswick, N.J.: Rutgers University Press, 2002).

31 See Patricia Hill Collins' *Black Feminist Thought* and *Black Sexual Politics*.

32 See Sophia Nelson's *Black Woman Redefined: Dispelling Myths and Discovering Fulfillment in the Age of Obama* (Dallas: BenBella Books, 2011) for a discussion of the ways that all black women have to deal with stereotypical representations of black womanhood.

33 See Janell Hobson's *Venus in the Dark: Blackness and Beauty in Popular Culture.* (New York: Routledge, 2005).

34 André Leon Talley, "Leading Lady," *Vogue*, March 2009.

35 Rachel L. Swarns, "First Lady in Control of Building Her Image," *New York Times*, April 24, 2009, http://www.nytimes.com/2009/04/25/us/politics/25michelle.html?ref=firstladiesus&pagewanted=print.

36 Talley, "Leading Lady," 429.

37 See Cotten and Springer's and *The Oprah Phenomenon* by Harris and Watson for a discussion of Oprah Winfrey's iconic status in popular culture.

38 This episode aired on ABC on June 18, 2008.

39 "Oprah Talks to Michelle Obama," *O*, April 2009, 140–47.

40 "Oprah Talks to Michelle Obama," 140–47.

41 "Here We Go!" preface to the article "Oprah Talks to Michelle Obama," *O*, April 2009, 33, emphasis added.

42 "Oprah Talks to Michelle Obama," 140, emphasis added.

43 "Oprah Talks to Michelle Obama," 141.

44 "Oprah Talks to Michelle Obama," 143.

45 "Oprah Talks to Michelle Obama," 143.

46 Jodi Kantor's *The Obamas* was released on January 10, 2012.

47 S. A. Miller, "Author Defends Michelle Portrait," *New York Post*, January 16, 2012, http://www.nypost.com/f/print/news/national/author_defends _michelle_portrait_GI4R0sYqQHNnqGTzw594WN; Alexander Abad-Santos, "Jodi Kantor Refutes Michelle Obama's 'Angry Black Woman'

148

Claim," *The Atlantic Wire*, January 12, 2012, http://www.theatlanticwire
.com/business/2012/01/jodi-kantor-refutes-michelle-obamas-angry
-black-woman-claim/47329/; Noreen Malone, "Jodi Kantor Talks about
White House Blowback on Her Book, *The Obamas*," *New York Magazine*,
January 13, 2012, http://nymag.com/daily/intel/2012/01/jodi-kantor-on
-white-house-the-obamas-blowback.html.

48 "Michelle Obama Denies She Is an 'Angry Black Woman' in White House,"
Boston Globe, January 12, 2012, http://www.bostonglobe.com/news/
nation/2012/01/12/michelle-obama-denies-she-angry-black-woman
-white-house/3686dDQgqPPm5Cm6J40pJJ/story.html; Catalina Camia,
"First Lady: Wrong to Paint Her as 'Angry Black Woman,'" *USA Today*,
January 11, 2012, http://content.usatoday.com/communities/theoval/
post/2012/01/michelle-obama-angry-black-woman-cbs-interview-/1;
"Michelle Obama: People Have Tried to Paint Me as 'Some Angry Black
Woman,'" *Huffington Post*, January 11, 2012, http://www.huffingtonpost
.com/2012/01/11/michelle-obama-the-obamas-jodi-kantor_n_1198747
.html?view=print&comm_ref=false.

49 "Michelle Obama: No Tension with Husband's Aides," *CBSNews.com*,
January 11, 2012, http://www.cbsnews.com/8301-505270_162-57356770/
michelle-obama-no-tension-with-husbands-aides/.

50 "Michelle Obama: No Tension."

51 "Michelle Obama: No Tension."

52 "Michelle Obama: No Tension."

53 "Michelle Obama: No Tension."

* The author would like to thank the following for images included in this
book: the Library of Congress; the Center for Archival Collections at Bowl-
ing Green State University; Photofest; the White House; EMEK Studios
and Erykah Badu for use of the Control Freaq logo and drawing of Erykah
Badu's black power fist; and Vaschelle André of Divine Photography for
use of the photograph of Alice Walker with a crown of flowers.

FILMOGRAPHY

Badass Supermama. Directed by Etang Inyang. Frameline, 1996. Videocassette.

Badu, Erykah. *On & On.* Universal, 1997. Music video.

Black Mama, White Mamma. Directed by Eddie Romero. 1973. Orion Home Video, 1998. Videocassette.

Brothers. Directed by Arthur Barron. 1977. Warner Home Video, 1996. Videocassette.

Coffy. Directed by Jack Hill. 1973. Orin Home Video, 1998. Videocassette.

The Color Purple. Directed by Steven Spielberg. 1985. Warner Home Video, 2003. DVD.

Foxy Brown. Directed by Jack Hill. 1974. MGM Home Entertainment, 2001. DVD.

Jackie Brown: Collector's Edition. Directed by Quentin Tarantino. 1997. Miramax Home Entertainment, 2002. DVD.

Ndegéocello, Me'shell. *If That's Your Boyfriend.* Maverick, 1994. Music video.

Ndegéocello, Me'shell. *Pocketbook.* Maverick, 2002. Music video.

Zabriskie Point. Directed by Michelangelo Antonioni. 1970. MGM/ UA Home Video, 1991. Videocassette.

BIBLIOGRAPHY

Abad-Santos, Alexander. "Jodi Kantor Refutes Michelle Obama's 'Angry Black Woman' Claim." *The Atlantic Wire*, January 12, 2012, http://www.theatlanticwire.com/business/2012/01/jodi-kantor-refutes-michelle-obamas-angry-black-woman-claim/47329/.

Alexander, Jackie. "Black Women in Hollywood." In Gledhill, *Stardom: Industry of Desire*, 45–54.

Alpern, Stanley B. *Amazons of Black Sparta: The Women Warriors of Dahomey.* 1998. Reprint, London: C. Hurst, 2011.

Anderson, Lisa M. *Mammies No More: The Changing Image of Black Women on Stage and Screen.* Lanham, Md.: Rowman & Littlefield, 1997.

"Angela Davis Case." *Newsweek*, October 26, 1970, 18–24.

"Angela Davis Talks about Her Future and Her Freedom." *Jet*, July 27, 1972, 54–57.

Aptheker, Bettina. *Women's Legacy: Essays on Race, Sex, and Class in America.* Amherst: University of Massachusetts Press, 1982.

Argetsinger, Amy, and Roxanne Roberts. "The Fist Couple: Giving a Big Bump to Authenticity." *Washington Post*, June 5, 2008, http://www.washingtonpost.com/wp-dyn/content/article/2008/06/04/AR2008060404521_pf.html.

152 Badu, Erykah. *Baduizm*. Universal, 1997. CD.

———. *Erykah Badu Live*. Universal, 1997. CD.

———. *Mama's Gun*. Motown, 2000. CD.

———. *Worldwide Underground*. Motown, 2003. CD.

Bederman, Gail. "'Civilization,' the Decline of Middle-Class Manliness, and Ida B. Wells's Antilynching Campaign (1892–94)." *Radical History Review* 52 (1992): 5–30.

Bell, Roseann P., Bettye J. Parker, and Beverly Guy-Sheftall. *Sturdy Black Bridges: Visions of Black Women in Literature*. Garden City, N.Y.: Anchor Books, 1979.

The Black Panther, August 16, 1969, 3.

Bobo, Jacqueline. *Black Feminist Cultural Criticism*. Malden, Mass.: Blackwell, 2001.

———. *Black Women as Cultural Readers*. New York: Columbia University Press, 1995.

Bogle, Donald. *Blacks in American Films and Television: An Illustrated Encyclopedia*. New York: Simon & Schuster, 1988.

———. *Toms, Coons, Mulattoes, Mammies, & Bucks: An Interpretive History of Blacks in American Films*. 3rd ed. New York: Continuum, 1996.

Boyd, Todd. *The New H.N.I.C.: The Death of Civil Rights and the Reign of Hip-Hop*. New York: New York University Press, 2002.

Brody, Jennifer DeVere. "The Return of Cleopatra Jones." *Signs: Journal of Women in Culture and Society* 25, no. 1 (1999): 91–121.

Brown, Elaine. *A Taste of Power: A Black Woman's Story*. New York: Pantheon Books, 1992.

Brown, Jeffrey A. *Dangerous Curves: Action Heroines, Gender, Fetishism, and Popular Culture*. Jackson: University Press of Mississippi, 2011.

Brown, Kimberly Nichele. *Writing the Black Revolutionary Diva: Women's Subjectivity and the Decolonizing Text*. Bloomington: Indiana University Press, 2010.

Bynoe, Yvonne. *Stand and Deliver: Political Activism, Leadership, and Hip Hop Culture*. Brooklyn, N.Y.: Soft Skull Press, 2004.

Byrd, Ayana, and Lori Tharps. *Hair Story: Untangling the Roots of Black Hair in America*. New York: St. Martin's, 2001.

Camia, Catalina. "First Lady: Wrong to Paint Her as 'Angry Black Woman.'" *USA Today*, January 11, 2012. http://content.us today.com/communities/theoval/post/2012/01/michelle -obama-angry-black-woman-cbs-interview-/1.

Campbell, Bebe Moore. "What Happened to the Afro?: Changing Hairstyles Reflect New Roles and New Definitions." *Ebony*, June 1982, 79–85.

"Chancellor in a Crossfire." *Time*, May 18, 1970, 83.

Christian, Barbara. *Black Women Novelists: The Development of a Tradition, 1892-1976*. Westport, Conn.: Greenwood Press, 1980.

Churchill, Ward, and Jim Vander Wall. *Agents of Repression: The FBI's Secret Wars against the Black Panther Party and the American Indian Movement*. 2nd ed. Cambridge, Mass.: South End, 2001.

Clark, Randall. *At a Theater or Drive-In Near You: The History, Culture and Politics of the American Exploitation Film*. New York: Garland, 1995.

Clarke, Cheryl. *"After Mecca": Women Poets and the Black Arts Movement*. New Brunswick, N.J.: Rutgers University Press, 2005.

Cleaver, Kathleen Neal. "Women, Power and Revolution." *New Political Science* 21, no. 2 (1999): 231–36.

Cloud, John. "Fist Bump." Number 4 in "The Top 10 Everything of 2008: The Top 10 Buzzwords." *Time*, November 3, 2008. http://www.time.com/time/specials/packages/article /0,28804,1855948_1864100_1864104,00.html.

Cocchi, John. "Edward and Mildred Lewis on Tour Promoting 'Brothers,' WB Release." *Box Office*, April 11, 1977, 5.

Cohen, Jon, and Michael D. Shear. "Poll Shows More Americans Think Obama Is a Muslim." *Washington Post*, August 19, 2010. http://www.washingtonpost.com/wp-dyn/content/ article/2010/08/18/AR2010081806913_pf.html.

Collins, Patricia Hill. *Black Feminist Thought: Knowledge, Consciousness, and the Politics of Empowerment*. Boston: Unwin Hyman, 1990.

———. *Black Sexual Politics: African Americans, Gender and the New Racism*. New York: Routledge, 2004.

154   ———. *Fighting Words: Black Women and the Search for Justice.* Minneapolis: University of Minnesota Press, 1998.

———. *From Black Power to Hip Hop: Racism, Nationalism, and Feminism.* Philadelphia: Temple University Press, 2006.

"Come Home Angela." *The Black Panther*, September 2, 1972, 3.

Cone, James H. *Martin & Malcolm & America: A Dream or a Nightmare.* Maryknoll, N.Y.: Orbis, 1991.

Cotten, Trystan, and Kimberly Springer. *Stories of Oprah: The Oprahfication of American Culture.* Jackson: University Press of Mississippi, 2010.

Crenshaw, Kimberlé. "Demarginalizing the Intersection of Race and Sex: A Black Feminist Critique of Antidiscrimination Doctrine, Feminist Theory, and Antiracist Politics." In *Feminism and Politics*, edited by A. Phillips, 314–43. New York: Oxford University Press, 1998..

Darling, Lynn. "Speaking the Unspoken." *Harper's Bazaar*, March 1994, 176–78.

Davis, Angela. "Afro Images: Politics, Fashion and Nostalgia." In *Soul: Black Power, Politics and Pleasure*, edited by M. Guillory and R. C. Green, 23–31. New York: New York University Press, 1998.

———. *Angela Davis: An Autobiography.* 1974. Reprint, New York: International Publishers, 1988.

———. "Black Nationalism: The Sixties and the Nineties." In Dent and Wallace, *Black Popular Culture*, 317–24.

———. *Blues Legacies and Black Feminism.* 1998. Reprint, New York: Vintage, 1999.

———. *If They Come in the Morning: Voices of Resistance.* New York: Signet, 1971.

DeLauretis, Teresa. *Alice Doesn't: Feminism, Semiotics, Cinema.* Bloomington: Indiana University Press, 1984.

DeLeon, Robert. "A Look at Angela Davis from Another Angle: Her Jail Cell." *Jet*, February 24, 1972, 8–14.

———. "A Revealing Report on Angela Davis' Fight for Freedom." *Jet*, November 18, 1971, 12–17.

———. "Angela Davis Works to Bring Change in Prison System."
Jet, May 16, 1974, 12–18.

Dent, Gina, and Michele Wallace, eds. *Black Popular Culture*. Seattle: Bay Press, 1992.

Dietrick, Katheryn Thomas. "A Reexamination of the Myth of the Black Matriarchy." *Journal of Marriage and Family* 37 (1975): 367–74.

Doane, Mary Ann. *Femme Fatales: Feminism, Film Theory, Psychoanalysis*. New York: Routledge, 1991.

Dobie, Kathy. "The Aggressives." *Vibe*, January 2003, 104–11.

Doss, Erika. "Revolutionary Art Is a Tool for Liberation: Emory Douglas and Protest Aesthetics at The Black Panther." *New Political Science* 21, no. 2 (1999): 245–59.

Douglas, Susan, and Meredith W. Michaels. *The Mommy Myth: The Idealization of Motherhood and How It Has Undermined All Women*. New York: Free Press, 2004.

DuCille, Ann. "The Shirley Temple of My Familiar." *Transition* 73 (1998): 10–32.

———. *Skin Trade*. Cambridge, Mass.: Harvard University Press, 1996.

Dunn, Stephane. *"Baad Bitches" & Sassy Supermamas: Black Power Action Films*. Urbana: University of Illinois Press, 2008.

———. "Foxy on My Mind: The Racialized Gendered Politics of Representation." In *Disco Divas: Women and Popular Culture in the 1970s*, edited by Sherrie A. Inness, 71–86. Philadelphia: University of Pennsylvania Press, 2003.

Dyer, Richard. *Stars*. 2nd ed. London: British Film Institute, 2002. Print.

Ellers, Cynthia. *Gentlemen and Amazons: The Myth of Matriarchal Prehistory, 1861-1900*. Berkeley: University of California Press, 2011.

Fergoso, Rosa Linda. "On the Road with Angela Davis." *Cultural Studies* 13, no. 2 (1999): 211–22.

Foster, Gwendolyn Audrey. *Captive Bodies: Postcolonial Subjectivity in Cinema*. Albany: State University of New York Press, 1999.

Friday, Nancy. *My Secret Garden: Women's Sexual Fantasies*. 1973. Reprint, New York: Pocket Books, 2008.

Gaines, Jane. "White Privilege and Looking Relations: Race and Gender in Feminist Film Theory." In *Issues in Film Criticism*, edited by Patricia Erens, 197–214. Bloomington: Indiana University Press, 1990.

Gates, Henry Louis, Jr., and K. A. Appiah, eds. *Alice Walker: Critical Perspectives Past and Present*. New York: Amistad Press, 1993.

Giddings, Paula J. *Ida: A Sword among Lions: Ida B. Wells and the Campaign against Lynching*. New York: HarperCollins, 2008.

———. *When and Where I Enter: The Impact of Black Women on Race and Sex in America*. 1984. Reprint, New York: HarperCollins, 1996.

Givhan, Robin. "Why a Hairstyle Made Headlines." *Washington Post*, April 7, 2006. http://www.washingtonpost.com/wp-dyn/content/article/2006/04/06/AR2006040602341_pf.html.

Gledhill, Christine, ed. *Stardom: Industry of Desire*. London: Routledge, 1991.

Gonzales, Michael. "Badu's Groove." *Essence*, August 1997, 90–92.

Graham, Tim. "Larry King Kept Asking Michelle Obama: 'Attack Dog' Palin Doesn't Make You Mad?" *Newsbusters.org*, October 10, 2008. http://newsbusters.org/blogs/tim-graham/2008/10/10/larry-king-kept-asking-michelle-obama-attack-dog-palin-doesnt-make-you-m.

Greaves, McLean. "Me'shell Ndegéocello: A Sista from Another Planet." *Essence*, September 1996, 95–96.

Gregory, Deborah. "Erykah Badu: Feel Her Flow." *Essence*, April 1997, 66.

Grier, Pam. *Foxy: My Life in Three Acts*. New York: Springboard Press, 2010.

Guerrero, Ed. *Framing Blackness: The African American Image in Film*. Philadelphia: Temple University Press, 1993.

Guy-Sheftall, Beverly. *Words of Fire: An Anthology of African-American Feminist Thought*. New York: New Press, 1995.

Halberstam, Judith. *Female Masculinity*. Durham, N.C.: Duke University Press, 1998.

Hammonds, Evelynn. "Black (W)holes and the Geometry of Black Female Sexuality." In *African American Literary Theory: A Reader*, edited by W. Napier, 482–97. New York: New York University Press, 2000.

Hankin, Kelly. *The Girls in the Back Room: Looking at the Lesbian Bar*. Minneapolis: University of Minnesota Press, 2002.

Harold, Claudrena N. "Running the Voodoo Down: An Interveiw with Meshell Ndegeocello." *PopMatters.com*, October 28, 2009. http://www.popmatters.com/pm/tools/print.

Harris, Jennifer, and Elwood Watson. *The Oprah Phenomenon*. Lexington: University Press of Kentucky, 2007.

Harris, Trudier. "On *The Color Purple*, Stereotypes, and Silence." *Black American Literature Forum* 18 (1984): 155–61.

Harris-Perry, Melissa V. *Sister Citizen: Shame, Stereotypes, and Black Women in America*. New Haven: Yale University Press, 2011.

Higginbotham, Evelyn Brooks. "African-American Women's History and the Metalanguage of Race." *Signs* 17, no. 21 (1992): 251–73.

Hine, Darlene Clark. "Rape and the Inner Lives of Black Women in the Middle West: Preliminary Thoughts on the Culture of Dissemblance." *Signs* 14 (1988): 912–20.

Hine, Darlene Clark, and Kathleen Thompson. *A Shining Thread of Hope: The History of Black Women in America*. New York: Broadway Books, 1998.

Hobson, Janell. *Venus in the Dark: Blackness and Beauty in Popular Culture*. New York: Routledge, 2005.

hooks, bell. *Black Looks: Race and Representation*. Cambridge, Mass.: South End, 1992.

———. "Reading and Resistance: *The Color Purple*." In Gates and Appiah, *Alice Walker: Critical Perspectives*, 284–95.

———. *Reel to Real: Race, Sex and Class at the Movies*. New York: Routledge, 1996.

Hull, Gloria T., Patricia Bell Scott, and Barbara Smith, eds. *All the Women Are White, All the Blacks Are Men, but Some of Us Are Brave: Black Women Studies*. New York: Feminist Press, 1982.

158 Humphries, Drew, ed. *Women, Violence, and the Media: Readings in Feminist Criminology.* Lebanon, N.H.: Northeastern University Press, 2009.

Ignatiev, Noel, and John Garvey. *Race Traitor.* New York: Routledge, 1996.

Jackson, George. *Soledad Brother: The Prison Letters of George Jackson.* 1970. Reprint, New York: Lawrence Hill Books, 1994.

James, Joy. "Angela Davis: A Life Committed to Liberation Praxis." *Abafazi: The Simmons College Review of Women of African Descent* 8, no. 1 (1997): 2–15.

———. *Resisting State Violence: Radicalism, Gender, and Race in U.S. Culture.* Minneapolis: University of Minnesota Press, 1996.

———. *Shadowboxing: Representations of Black Feminist Politics.* New York: St. Martin's, 1999.

James, Stanlie Myrise, Frances Smith Foster, and Beverly Guy-Sheftall. *Still Brave: The Evolution of Black Women's Studies.* New York: Feminist Press, 2009.

Jeffries, Judson L. *Huey P. Newton: The Radical Theorist.* Jackson: University Press of Mississippi, 2002.

Jones, Charles E., ed. *The Black Panther Party Reconsidered.* Baltimore: Black Classic Press, 1998.

Jones, Lisa. *Bulletproof Diva: Tales of Race, Sex, and Hair.* New York: Anchor Books/Doubleday, 1994.

Jordan, Winthrop D. *White over Black: American Attitudes toward the Negro, 1550-1812.* 2nd ed. Chapel Hill: University of North Carolina Press, 2012.

Kantor, Jodi. *The Obamas.* New York: Penguin, 2012.

Kaplow, Susan. "Behind the Scenes with Erykah Badu." *Seventeen,* June 1997, 108.

Keeling, Kara. "'Ghetto Heaven': *Set It Off* and the Valorization of Black Lesbian Butch-Femme Sociality." *The Black Scholar* 33, no. 1 (2003): 33–46.

———. *The Witches Flight: The Cinematic, the Black Femme, and the Image of Common Sense.* Durham, N.C.: Duke University Press, 2007.

Kincaid, Jamaica. "Pam Grier: The Mocha Mogul of Hollywood." *Ms.* August 1975, 49–53.

Koppelman, Alex. "Fox News Calls Michelle Obama 'Obama's Baby Mama.'" *Salon.com*, June 11, 2008. http://www.salon.com/2008/06/12/fox_obama/.

Koven, Mikel J. *The Pocket Essential Blaxploitation Films.* Harpenden, UK: Pocket Essentials, 2001.

LeBlanc-Ernest, Angela D. "'The Most Qualified Person to Handle the Job': Black Panther Party Women, 1966–1971." In Jones, *Black Panther Party Reconsidered*, 305–34.

Lee, Shayne. *Erotic Revolutionaries: Black Women, Sexuality, and Popular Culture.* Lanham, Md.: Hamilton Books, 2010.

Lee, Valerie. *Granny Midwives & Black Women Writers: Double-Dutched Readings.* New York: Routledge, 1996.

Lipsitz, George. "Genre Anxiety and Racial Representation in 1970s Cinema." In *Refiguring American Film Genres: History and Theory*, edited by Nick Browne, 208–32. Berkeley: University of California Press, 1998

Lorde, Audre. *The Cancer Journals.* San Francisco: Aunt Lute Books, 1980.

———. *Sister Outsider: Essays and Speeches by Audre Lorde.* Berkeley, Calif.: Crossing Press, 1984.

———. *Zami: A New Spelling of My Name.* Berkeley, Calif.: Crossing Press, 1982.

Lubiano, Wahneema. "Black Ladies, Welfare Queens, and State Minstrels: Ideological War by Narrative Means." In Morrison, *Race-ing Justice, En-gendering Power*, 323–63.

Malone, Noreen. "Jodi Kantor Talks about White House Blowback on Her Book, *The Obamas.*" *New York Magazine*, January 13, 2012. http://nymag.com/daily/intel/2012/01/jodi-kantor-on-white-house-the-obamas-blowback.html.

Marvin, Thomas F. "'Preachin' the Blues': Bessie Smith's Secular Religion and Alice Walker's *The Color Purple.*" *African American Review* 28 (1994): 411–21.

160 Matthews, Tracye. "'No One Ever Asks, What a Man's Place in the Revolution Is': Gender and the Politics of the Black Panther Party 1966–1971." In Jones, *Black Panther Party Reconsidered*, 267–304.

Mayne, Judith. "Feminist Film Theory and Criticism." *Signs* 11, no. 1 (1985): 81–100.

———. *Framed: Lesbians, Feminists, and Media Culture*. Minneapolis: University of Minnesota Press, 2000.

McDowell, Deborah. *"The Changing Same": Black Women's Literature, Criticism, and Theory*. Bloomington: Indiana University Press, 1995.

McGinley, Ann C. "Hillary Clinton, Sarah Palin, and Michelle Obama: Performing Gender, Race, and Class on the Campaign Trail." *Scholarly Works*, paper 171, 2009. http://scholars.law.unlv.edu/facpub/171.

McIver, Joel. *Erykah Badu: The First Lady of Neo-Soul*. London: Sanctuary, 2002.

"Michelle Obama Denies She Is an 'Angry Black Woman' in White House." *Boston Globe*, January 12, 2012. http://www.bostonglobe.com/news/nation/2012/01/12/michelle-obama-denies-she-angry-black-woman-white-house/3686dDQgqPPm5Cm6J40pJJ/story.html.

"Michelle Obama: No Tension with Husband's Aides." *CBSNews.com*, January 11, 2012. http://www.cbsnews.com/8301-505270_162-57356770/michelle-obama-no-tension-with-husbands-aides/.

"Michelle Obama: People Have Tried to Paint Me as 'Some Angry Black Woman.'" *Huffington Post*, January 11, 2012. http://www.huffingtonpost.com/2012/01/11/michelle-obama-the-obamas-jodi-kantor_n_1198747.html?view=print&comm_ref=false.

Miller, S. A. "Author Defends Michelle Portrait." *New York Post*, January 16, 2012. http://www.nypost.com/f/print/news/national/author_defends_michelle_portrait_GI4R0sYqQHNnqGTzw594WN.

Moraga, Cherríe, and Gloria Anzaldúa. *This Bridge Called My Back: Writings by Radical Women of Color*. New York: Kitchen Table Women of Color Press, 1981.

Morgan, Joan. *When Chickenheads Come Home to Roost: My Life as a Hip-Hop Feminist*. New York: Simon & Schuster, 1999.

Morrison, Toni, ed. *Race-ing Justice, En-gendering Power: Essays on Anita Hill, Clarence Thomas, and the Construction of Social Reality*. New York: Pantheon Books, 1992.

Morthland, John. "The Voice of Amerykah." *Texas Monthly*, May 1997, 58.

Morton, Patricia. *Disfigured Images: The Historical Assault on Afro-American Women*. Westport, Conn.: Greenwood Press, 1991.

Moynihan, Daniel Patrick. *The Negro Family: The Case for National Action*. Washington, D.C.: U.S. Department of Labor, Office of Policy Planning and Research, 1965.

Mullings, Leith. "Image, Ideology, and Women of Color." In *Women of Color in U.S. Society*, edited by Maxine Baca Zinn and Bonnie Thornton Dill, 265–90. Philadelphia: Temple University Press, 1994.

Mulvey, Laura. "Afterthoughts on 'Visual Pleasure and Narrative Cinema' Inspired by *Dual in the Sun*." In Penley, *Feminism and Film Theory*, 69–79.

———. "Visual Pleasure and Narrative Cinema." In Penley, *Feminism and Film Theory*, 57–68.

Murch, Donna Jean. *Living for the City: Migration, Education and the Rise of the Black Panther Party in Oakland, California*. Chapel Hill: University of North Carolina Press, 2010.

Murray, Sonia. "Song for a Friend." *Atlanta Journal-Constitution*, August 12, 1993.

Nadel, Alan. "Reading the Body: *Meridian* and the Archeology of Self." In Gates and Appiah, *Alice Walker: Critical Perspectives*, 155–67.

Ndegéocello, Me'shell. *Cookie: The Anthropological Mixtape*. Maverick, 2002. CD.

———. *Plantation Lullabies*. Maverick, 1993. CD.

162   Neal, Mark Anthony. *Songs in the Key of Black Life: A Rhythm and Blues Nation.* New York: Routledge, 2003.

Nelson, Sophia. *Black Woman Redefined: Dispelling Myths and Discovering Fulfillment in the Age of Obama.* Dallas: BenBella Books, 2011.

Newton, Huey P. *To Die for the People: The Writings of Huey P. Newton.* Edited by Toni Morrison and Elaine Brown. San Francisco: City Lights Books, 2009.

Omi, Michael, and Howard Winant. *Racial Formation in the United States from the 1960s to the 1980s.* New York: Routledge & Kegan Paul, 1986.

"Oprah Talks to Michelle Obama." *O,* April 2009, 140–47.

Painter, Nell Irvin. "Representing Truth: Sojourner Truth's Knowing and Becoming Known." *Journal of American History* 81, no. 2 (1994): 461–92.

———. *Sojourner Truth: A Life, a Symbol.* New York: Norton, 1997.

"Pam Grier Finds Fame in Black Movie Films." *Jet,* August 9, 1973, 58–61.

Parks, Gregory S., and Quinetta M. Roberson. "Michelle Obama: 'The Darker Side' of Presidential Spousal Involvement and Activism." *Cornell Law Faculty Working Papers,* paper 39, 2008. http://scholarship.law.cornell.edu/clsops_papers/39.

Parks, Sheri. *Fierce Angels: The Strong Black Woman in American Life and Culture.* New York: One World, 2010.

"The Path of Angela Davis." *Life,* September 11, 1970, 20D–27.

Penley, Constance, ed. *Feminism and Film Theory.* New York: Routledge, 1988.

Perry, Gerald. *Quentin Tarantino: Interviews.* Jackson: University Press of Mississippi, 1998.

Perry, Imani. *Prophets of the Hood: Politics and Poetics in Hip Hop.* Durham, N.C.: Duke University Press, 2004.

Porterfield, Christopher. "Recycling Job." *Time,* April 18, 1977, 82.

Pough, Gwendolyn D. *Check It While I Wreck It: Black Womanhood, Hip-Hop Culture, and the Public Sphere.* Boston: Northeastern University Press, 2004.

Prince, Althea. *The Politics of Black Women's Hair.* London: Insomniac Press, 2009.

Projansky, Sarah. *Watching Rape: Film and Television in Postfeminist Culture.* New York: New York University Press, 2001.

Reed, Ishmael. *Airing Dirty Laundry.* New York: Perseus, 1995.

Robinson, Cedric J. "Blaxploitation and the Misrepresentation of Liberation." *Race and Class: A Journal for Black and Third World Liberation* 40, no. 1 (1998): 1–12.

Rooks, Noliwe M. *Hair Raising: Beauty, Culture, and African American Women.* New Brunswick, N.J.: Rutgers University Press, 1996.

Rose, Tricia. *Black Noise: Rap Music and Black Culture in Contemporary America.* Hanover, N.H.: University Press of New England, 1994.

———. "Cultural Survivalisms and Marketplace Subversions: Black Popular Culture and Politics into the Twenty-First Century." In *Language, Rhythm, and Sound: Black Popular Cultures into the Twenty-First Century,* edited by Joseph Adjaye and Adrianne R. Andrews, 259–72. Pittsburgh: University of Pittsburgh Press, 1997.

Rosen, Ruth. *The World Split Open: How the Modern Women's Movement Changed America.* 2nd ed. New York: Penguin, 2000.

Salvatore, Diane. "The Presidential Race Part I: The Obamas." *Ladies' Home Journal,* September 2008, 121–31.

Samuels, Allison. "What Michelle Means to Us." *Newsweek,* December 1, 2008, 32.

Saulny, Susan. "Michelle Obama Thrives in Campaign Trenches." *New York Times,* February 14, 2008. http://www.nytimes.com/2008/02/14/us/politics/14michelle.html?pagewanted=print.

Shakur, Assata. *Assata: An Autobiography.* 1987. Reprint, Chicago: Lawrence Hill Books, 2001.

Sims, Yvonne D. *Women of Blaxploitation: How the Black Action Film Heroine Changed American Popular Culture.* Jefferson, N.C.: McFarland, 2006.

164 Smith, Barbara. *Homegirls: A Black Feminist Anthology*. New York: Kitchen Table Women of Color Press, 1983.

———. "A Press of Our Own: Kitchen Table: Women of Color Press." *Frontiers: A Journal of Women's Studies* 10, no. 3 (1989): 11–13.

———. "Towards a Black Feminist Criticism." In Hull, Scott, and Smith, *All the Women Are White*, 157–75.

Smith, Jesse Carney. *Images of Blacks in American Culture: A Reference Guide to Information Sources*. Westport, Conn.: Greenwood Press, 1988.

Smith, Shawn Michelle. *American Archives: Gender, Race, and Class in Visual Culture*. Princeton, N.J.: Princeton University Press, 1999.

Smith-Shomade, Beretta E. *Shaded Lives: African-American Women and Television*. New Brunswick, N.J.: Rutgers University Press, 2002.

Sontag, Susan. *On Photography*. New York: Picador, 1973.

Stacey, Jackie. "Feminine Fascinations: Forms of Identification in Star–Audience Relations." In Gledhill, *Stardom: Industry of Desire*, 141–63.

Staples, Robert. "The Myth of the Black Matriarchy." *The Black Scholar* 1 (1970): 9–16.

Swarns, Rachel L. "First Lady in Control of Building Her Image." *New York Times*, April 24, 2009. http://www.nytimes.com/2009/04/25/us/politics/25michelle.html?ref=firstladiesus&pagewanted=print.

Talley, André Leon. "Leading Lady." *Vogue*, March 2009, 428–35.

Tarantino, Quentin. *Jackie Brown: A Quentin Tarantino Screenplay*. New York: Miramax Books, 1997.

Tasker, Yvonne. *Spectacular Bodies: Gender, Genre and the Action Cinema*. London: Routledge, 1993.

Tate, Claudia. *Psychoanalysis and Black Novels: Desire and the Protocols of Race*. New York: Oxford University Press, 1998.

Thompson, Cordell S. "Angela Davis Case Puts Justice on Trial." *Jet*, May 6, 1971, 44–49.

BIBLIOGRAPHY

Truth, Sojourner. *Narrative of Sojourner Truth: Unabridged*. 1850. Reprint, Mineola, N.Y.: Dover, 1997.

Waldschmidt-Nelson, Britta. *Dreams and Nightmares: Martin Luther King Jr., Malcolm X, and the Struggle for Black Equality in America*. Gainesville: University Press of Florida, 2012.

Walker, Alice. *The Color Purple*. Orlando, Fla.: Harcourt, 1982.

———. "'I Am a Renegade, an Outlaw, a Pagan'—Author, Poet, and Activist Alice Walker in Her Own Words." Interview by Amy Goodman. *DemocracyNow.org*, February 13, 2006, http://www.democracynow.org/2006/2/13/i_am_a_renegade_an_outlaw.

———. *In Search of Our Mothers' Gardens: Womanist Prose*. New York: Harcourt Brace Jovanovich, 1984.

———. *Meridian*. New York: Harcourt Brace Jovanovich, 1976.

———. *Revolutionary Petunias & Other Poems*. New York: Harcourt Brace Jovanovich, 1973.

Walker, Beverly. "Michelangelo and the Leviathan: The Making of *Zabriskie Point*." *Film Comment*, September–October 1992, 36.

Walker, Susannah. *Style and Status: Selling Beauty to African American Women, 1920-1975*. Lexington: University Press of Kentucky, 2007.

Wall, Wendy. "Lettered Bodies and the Corporeal Texts." In Gates and Appiah, *Alice Walker: Critical Perspectives*, 261–74.

Wallace, Michele. *Black Macho and the Myth of Superwoman*. 1978. Reprint, London: Verso, 1999.

———. *Invisibility Blues: From Pop to Theory*. London: Verso, 1990.

Walters, Suzanna Danuta. "Caged Heat: The (R)evolution of Women-in-Prison Films." In *Reel Knockouts: Violent Women in the Movies*, edited by Martha McCaughey and Neal King, 106–23. Austin: University of Texas Press, 2001.

Watkins, S. Craig. *Representing: Hip-Hop Culture and the Production of Black Cinema*. Chicago: University of Chicago Press, 1998.

Watts, Eric King. "The Female Voice in Hip-Hop: An Exploration into the Potential of the Erotic Appeal." In *Centering*

166 *Ourselves: African American Feminist and Womanist Studies of Discourse*, edited by Marsha Houston and Olga Idriss Davis, 187–214. Cresskill, N.J.: Hampton Press, 2002.

"'Welfare Queen' Becomes Issue in Reagan Campaign." *New York Times*, February 15, 1976, 51. http://select.nytimes.com/gst/abstract.html?res=FA0614FB395910728DDDAC0994DA405B868BF1D3&scp=2&sq=Welfare%20Queen%20and%20Reagan%20Campaign&st=cse.

Wells, Ida B. *Southern Horrors and Other Writings: The Anti-Lynching Campaign of Ida B. Wells, 1892–1900*. Edited by Jacqueline Jones Royster. Boston: Beford Books, 1997.

Welter, Barbara. "The Cult of True Womanhood: 1820–1860." *American Quarterly* 18, no. 2 (1966): 151–74.

Westbrook, Alonzo. *Hip Hoptionary: A Dictionary of Hip Hop Terminology*. New York: Harlem Moon, 2002.

Westfall, Sandra Sobieraj. "Michelle Obama: We're Home." *People* 71, no. 9, March 9, 2009, 112–18.

White, Deborah Gray. *Ar'n't I a Woman? Female Slaves in the Plantation South*. New York: Norton, 1999.

White, Patricia. *Uninvited: Classical Hollywood Cinema and Lesbian Representability*. Bloomington: Indiana University Press, 1999.

"White-on-White Jury for Angela Too!" *The Black Panther*, November 20, 1971, 2.

Willis, Sharon. *High Contrast: Race and Gender in Contemporary Hollywood Film*. Durham, N.C.: Duke University Press, 1997.

Wing, Adrien. *Critical Race Feminism: A Reader*. 2nd ed. New York: New York University Press, 2003.

Wright, Michelle M. *Becoming Black: Creating Identity in the African Diaspora*. Durham, N.C.: Duke University Press, 2004.

York, Wendy Jill. "Luck Star." *The Advocate*, October 19, 1993, 58–60.

INDEX

2008 Election, 108

abolition, 7–8, 10
activism, activist(s), 5, 7, 11–12,
15–16, 19, 25, 28–29, 35, 39, 42, 45,
47, 54–55, 58, 67–68, 78–80, 82, 84,
88–89, 92, 130n7
actresses in blaxploitation film, 47, 57,
63, 644
The Advocate magazine, 143
Afrekete, 83–84
African American men, 16, 55, 57,
92–93
African American or black womanhood, 2, 5, 7–8, 10–11, 13, 60, 67, 69,
84, 88, 102, 115, 117, 121, 133, 136,
138, 142, 147
African American women, 1, 5, 8,
10–12, 16–17, 34, 46–47, 49, 52–53,
55–56, 58–60, 64, 65, 67–69, 72–74,
76–77, 85, 88, 92–94, 98, 100, 106,
110–11, 117, 128, 130, 132, 136, 139,
144, 146
Afro, 15, 17–19, 21, 36, 51, 61, 67, 78, 89,
95, 107, 110, 112–13, 130–31, 136, 139
Afrocentric or black aesthetic, 47,
88–91, 95, 106,131n2, 143n11

agency, 59, 88, 101, 106
Aggressives, 102, 145n45
Alice Walker, 12, 67–69, 74, 84–85,
87, 95, 128, 139n3, 139nn5–8,
142nn54–55
allegiance, 6, 53, 59
amazon(s), amazonian, 69–71, 82–83,
139, 140
Americans, 4, 6–7, 10, 15–16, 35, 46, 57,
88, 92–93, 104, 114, 130n6, 132n6,
135n2, 135n4, 143n5, 146n12
antiracist, 55, 68, 129n5
anxieties, 11, 17, 23, 44, 46–47, 52–53,
65, 114, 121, 123, 126
archetypes, archetypal, 11, 65, 136n13
artistic, 97, 139n3, 142n52
artists, 65, 67, 69, 84, 87, 89, 93–94, 106,
118, 142n4, 143n11, 144n35
assimilated, assimilation, 6, 12, 15
audience(s), 40, 45–46, 51, 53, 57, 60,
62, 74, 76, 85, 92–93, 96, 104–5,
135n3
authentic (-ity), 39, 114, 146n16
autobiographical, autobiography, 94,
132n9,133n28

baby mama, 115–16, 147n24

ICONIC

INDEX

INDEX

INDEX